THE SAGA OF BLACK NAVY VETERANS OF WORLD WAR II

AN AMERICAN TRIUMPH

JAMES S. PETERS, II

THE SAGA OF BLACK NAVY VETERANS OF WORLD WAR II
AN AMERICAN TRIUMPH

JAMES S. PETERS, II

157309-123-5

cip info

To the hundreds of World War II Black Navy Veterans who served our country on land, on sea and in ammunition depots, in particular, to those that gave their lives at Port Chicago, California.

Contents

Chapter 1
Segregation in the Navy: The Beginning of the End 1

Chapter 2
The Results of Segregation and Discrimination 9

Chapter 3
The Saga of Black Navy Veterans of World War II: An American Trumph 23

Chapter 4
Organizing Black World War II Navy Veterans of Great Lakes: The Beginning—September 1982 55

Appendix 1
The Special Training Program 61

Appendix 2
A Transcript of the Minutes of the Reunion of Band Members of Great Lakes Naval Training Center, Southern Illinois University, Carbondale, Illinois—Spring 1973 85

Appendix 3
World War II Black Navy Veterans of Great Lakes: Constitution, Correspondence, Press Releases, Etc. .. 105

Appendix 4
World War II Black Navy Veterans Celebrate the Fiftieth Anniversary of Entrance into General Service of the U.S. Navy—June 20, 1992 139

The Last Word 153

The Author 155

Index 157

Preface

Prior to entering the United States Navy I was a social and economic pacifist. I abhorred war and all its trappings; I did not feel comfortable with the military, and in particular, the way it was structured along social, economic and color lines. Then too, being a second class citizen I did not feel that I should be made to fight and kill for human rights that as a Negro, I had never enjoyed. However, I believed so strongly in democracy and freedom that I felt obligated to aid in the struggle against fascism by working in a defense plant; Colts Patent Firearms, Hartford, Connecticut, while writing my master's degree thesis in psychology at Hartford Seminary where I was a student.

My appeal for conscientious objector status (C.O.) through the draft board in Hartford to Selective Service Headquarters, Washington, D.C. was turned down on the basis that I was not a minister or theology student; therefore, I had to either go to jail or into the Army. This ruling came in June 1942 following my graduation in May and prior to my marriage. This placed me in a double bind. I married Marie E. Ferguson, June 25, 1942. We were married by Father A. E. Lambert in Saint Monica's Episcopal Church, Hartford, Connecticut. I took my bride to 25 Warren Terrace, West Hartford where we mulled over my decision to enter the army or the federal prison, Danbury.

A decision was made to volunteer for the United States Navy's general service as a Welfare Worker, Assistant to the Chaplain after receiving a brochure about the Navy from my wife's brother-in-law who was a Chief Petty Officer, Navy

Recruiter, in North Carolina. His name was Harold Adams, a former professor of business at Johnson C. Smith College, a Presbyterian College for Negro boys, Charlotte, North Carolina.

I enlisted in the Navy, November 12, 1942 in Baltimore, Maryland but was denied my rating of Welfare Worker which is a specialist rating. However, I was later rated Specialist Teacher (Psychologist) while a member of ship's company, Great Lakes Naval Training Center for over three years. It was great duty! The rest is history!

—James S. Peters, II
Storrs, Connecticut

Acknowledgments

It is impossible to name all of the wonderful people who encouraged and/or assisted me in the development of this work. However, a special note of thanks is to Professor Janet Macy of The University of Minnesota; James Howard of Hyannis, Massachusetts; Huel D. Perkins, Sr., and Walter Mines, Baton Rouge, Louisiana; Joan Soucier of Coventry, Connecticut; Groves Conference on Marriage and Family; and last, but in no way least, officers and members of Black Navy Veterans of World War II.

Special thanks to my editor, Diane Spencer Hume, without her help this book would not have been possible.

I am deeply indebted to all of the above and many more.

CHAPTER 1

SEGREGATION IN THE NAVY: THE BEGINNING OF THE END

A historical meeting of Black Navy Veterans who had served at the Great Lakes Naval Training Center took place in Chicago, Illinois from Thursday, June 18 to Sunday, June 21, 1992. They were commemorating the 50th anniversary of President Franklin D. Roosevelt signing the executive order opening up general service to Negro recruits who qualified to enter the United States Navy in April 1942. Although the recruits were initially only alloweded shore duty, this signified the beginning of the end of segregation in the U.S. Navy.

The United States and her allies had been at war with the Axis power, Germany, Italy and Japan for over a year and there was an overall manpower shortage, particularly for the Navy. Prior to the year 1942 Blacks could serve in the Navy only as mess attendants and stewards. With the opening of general service they could be trained to become able bodied seamen, signalmen, quartermasters, gunnersmates, radio mechanics, yeomen, pharmacistmates, electronic technicians, aviation metalsmiths, shore patrolmen, athletic specialists, teachers, classification specialists, etc., but not as commissioned officers. Blacks could only become petty officers and that, with great effort no matter how well-educated or to what extent their experience. Commissioning of Blacks came much later when thirteen were commissioned.

Camp Robert Smalls

In June 1942 a separate camp was established for Negro recruits on a segregated basis at The United States Naval Training Center, Great Lakes, Illinois, about forty miles north of Chicago. This camp was named Robert Smalls in honor of a Black civil war hero.

Robert Smalls was born the son of slaves in Beaufort, South Carolina. He later moved to Charleston where, eventually, he was pressed into the service of the Confederate Navy. Smalls joined the crew of the Planter in 1861. When in 1862, he delivered the Planter to the Federal forces, they made him a pilot in the United States Navy with the rank of Captain. He was later promoted to Commander. Smalls was a delegate to the State Constitutional Convention in 1868, and served in the House of Representatives of the State of South Carolina. He later became a State Senator and was eventually elected to Congress where he served from 1875 to 1887.[1]

D. W. Armstrong, White, a Captain in the Navy reserve who was a graduate of Annapolis and a descendent of General Armstrong a founder of Hampton Institute, a school for Blacks in Virginia, was made Commander of the Unit at Camp Smalls. He was a fair leader who wanted the Black sailors to do well. He accepted the Navy's segregation and discrimination against Blacks, but worked hard to make things better for them. For example, aside from administering the recruit training program of a military nature he helped to establish these major units:

> Classification
> Physical Education
> Band
> Special Training (education)

Segregation in the Navy: The Beginning of the End

Commander Armstrong had a strong sense of duty to his country and to the men under his command. His grandfather or great grandfather had led a Black union regiment during the Civil War. We were taught to sing one of General Armstrong's regimental songs: *They Look Like Men*. It goes like this:

> *They look like men; they look like men!*
> *They look like men of war!*
> *All dressed in, their uniform, they look*
> *like men of war!*

In November and December 1943 (eight months after Commander Armstrong had visited Washington and had reaffirmed his segregation program), the educational planning officer of all the service schools made an intensive survey of the Negro service schools. He found much room for improvement, and set about making desirable changes. Lack of lesson plans, too much lecturing, little use of job sheets, unwise selection and use of training aids by some instructors and too much shifting of instructor personnel from one assignment to another, were among the faults found. The planning officer pointed out the need for an analysis of student failures with a view of doing remedial work. He further urged the selection of good supervisors and teachers for the Negro schools. This officer believed that the Negro schools were inefficient in that there were only four or five students in some classes. Segregation in the service school command, he found, was a useless luxury in maintaining two sets of units that could have been adequately consolidated and handled by one. Attention was thus focused upon this under-use of personnel, facilities and equipment. The White schools were being used to capacity while only a portion of the "separate but equal" facilities of the segregated unit were being utilized.

The obvious remedy for the inefficiency of very small classes and the over-all wastage involved, was to integrate the few Negroes with White students 'across the tracks.' When such integration was introduced on a small scale in 1944, the experiment proved an immediate success. A few Negroes were placed in the chief commissary stewards,' gunners' mates,' fire controlmen's, torpedomen's and electricians' mates' schools. A survey established soon after proved that the Negro students were well liked and well treated, did well in their classes and had no complaints to make. A few had been teased upon arrival but not enough to cause undue distress. (United States Naval Administration in World War II, *BuPers*.)

Lack of free competition resulted in social inefficiency and rigid class, caste and race distinctions which hampered progress. It has been interesting to note that in the early days of segregated recruit training, disciplinary problems were often acute, and many were of a serious nature. Under the segregated system, disciplinary problems of Negroes tended to fall into categories implied as "peculiar to Negroes." Chief among these were marijuana cigarette smoking, tardy returnees from liberty, and incidents of sleeping on duty. But in the program of integrated training of the service schools, disciplinary problems were of the same nature as Whites, and none could be ascribed as "peculiar to Negroes."

During the later stage of Negro training at Great Lakes, the view that segregation was a mistake and totally undesirable gradually began to take hold. Segregation seems to have been

Segregation in the Navy: The Beginning of the End

taken for granted at Great Lakes under the leadership of Commander Armstrong in 1942, but there were few proponents of the pattern in 1945. The success of the 1944 integration experiment in the service schools spelled doom to the program of segregation and was perhaps the major factor in increasing the demand for integration. Contributing factors, too, were patent inefficiency of segregation and the need for the facilities, staff and equipment available in all phases of training but not used to capacity.

In September 1944, Commander Armstrong was detached. His training program had shrunk rapidly in the spring and summer of 1944 until there remained only 3,000 Negro recruits in training. Officers who succeeded Armstrong in command of the Negro units at Great Lakes found few of the difficulties that had beset the Commander when the program was new and expanding or in his efforts to firmly establish recruit training on a segregated basis. By May 1945, there were only 1,888 Negro recruits at the base (719 of them being illiterates in the Special Training Unit), as compared with 13,500 in training in February 1944. The Negro service schools disappeared as a separate entity entirely. Not more than a dozen Negro service school students remained, and these were integrated in the White service schools; one or two in a class in several schools.

According to Commander Dennis Nelson[3] the disbanding of the separate camps for Negroes at Great Lakes signaled a change in naval policy. It foreshadowed the end of segregation in the military in 1948 when Truman became president. Lessons learned through experiences at all three Negro units at Great Lakes paved the way to integration.

In May 1945, Captain Bond, commanding officer of the service schools, recommended to Commodore Emmett the integration of the aviation metalsmiths' school with a similar school at Norman, Oklahoma. During the same month, Commodore Emmett, commandant of the training center, recommended to the Bureau of Naval Personnel the integration of Negro illiterates at Camp Peary, Williamsburg, Virginia, by means of companies within regiments. The Bureau of Naval Personnel not only accepted the recommendations but went so far as to issue, in June 1945, a notable directive calling for total integration and assimilation of recruit training units and special training units at other stations as well. Commander Turek, commanding officer of recruit training, had misgivings about integration, but his relief, Captain Penny, carried out the bureau's directives immediately and encountered no difficulties. When asked what allowance he intended making for the supposed inferiority of Negroes, he replied, emphatically, "None!"

Captain Penny integrated recruits and recruit units by companies in July 1945, putting two Negro companies with four White companies in the same battalion. Before long he was gratified to see a Negro company win the highest battalion awards. Then, in August 1945, just before the end of the war, he shifted to complete integration, with eight to ten Negroes assigned to a company. In a short time a Negro was voted as honor man of his company.

The continued success of integration in the service schools, and the success Captain Penny experienced with recruit training integration on a larger scale, encouraged the top administrative officers (Commodore Emmett, Captains Freeman, Penny and Bond) to speak approvingly and enthusiastically of the new program. Captain Bond heartily concurred that: "Segregation was an egregious error. It was un-American and inefficient — a waste of money and manpower." (United States Naval Administration in World War II, *BuPers*.)

Segregation in the Navy: The Beginning of the End

Armstrong admitted at the close of the war that integration should have been instituted at the beginning. Thus, after much bitterness, multiple problems and wastage, the Navy found that integration of personnel in training and utilization was far more practical, desirable and efficient than a system of segregation that only tended to develop friction, create misunderstanding, lower morale and help perpetuate traditional theories of inferiority. In an environment where men of all races had to work, fight and live together in close quarters with little chance for complete physical separation, as is typical aboard ship, there was little, if any, justification for segregation and separation in their training.

Following this bold and "revolutionary" venture, problems encountered by the Bureau of Naval Personnel in the handling and development of its Negro personnel were met fearlessly and intelligently through numerous directives concerning the training, utilization, advancement and maintenance of mixed units, afloat and ashore.

Wars and conflicts of global proportions tend to prove that the military situation calls for a more complete integration of the Negro in our fighting forces. In effect, this means nothing less than mixed and integrated military units. The experience of the Army, though on a far more limited basis than the Navy, indicates that Americans of White and Negro skins can serve harmoniously and cooperatively in the military services together if given the chance.

Endnotes

[1] Peter M. Bergman, *The Chronological History of the Negro in America* (New York: Harper and Row, 1969, pp. 167-168).

[2] S.A. Floyd, "The Great Lakes Experience 1942-1945," Southern Illinois University at Carbondale, p. 973, p. 1.

[3] D. Nelson. *The Integration of The Negro Into the U.S. Navy.* Farrar and Young, New York, 1951, pp. 46-49.

CHAPTER 2

THE RESULTS OF SEGREGATION AND DISCRIMINATION

The Port Chicago "Mutiny"

During the early years of the war, Negro general service men, both class "A" school graduates and illiterates, were predominant in the personnel of ammunition depots and naval magazines. On July 17, 1944, two ships loading ammunition exploded at the docks at Port Chicago, a small town on San Francisco Bay. Over 300 persons were killed outright, and several hundred injured. About 250 of the men killed were Negro seamen loading the ships. Nine White officers in charge of the loading, 70 members of the mixed crews of the two ships, 15 Coast Guardsmen, and numerous civilians were also killed. Most of the injured were Negro stevedores in their barracks a mile from the dock at the time of the explosion.

On August 9, 1944, the survivors, who were scattered about the various camps, were assembled at Vallejo, a few miles from Port Chicago, with the view to resuming the loading. The men, however, were reluctant to return to work. Various reasons were cited by the principal cause was fear of another disaster.

After three days of persuasion and urging, the commandant of the naval district was called in, but his efforts in appealing to the men were largely unavailing. Of the 400 men at hand, 258 were definitely unable to calm their fears, and they were put in virtual confinement on a barge at the docks.

The chaplain and others continued for several days to persuade and interview the men, with the result that all but 44 of the 258 expressed willingness to resume the loading. These 44, plus 6 others who balked after a few days at work, were formally charged with mutiny.

On September 14, 1944, the "mutineers" were put on trial before a naval courts martial. The trial lasted approximately six weeks, ending on October 24, 1944, with a verdict of guilty for all: Three weeks later they were sentenced from eight to fifteen years at hard labor, plus dishonorable discharge from the service. The initial sentence in each case was fifteen years, but Rear Admiral Carleton Wright, commandant of the district, ruled that 40 of the men were entitled, because of mitigating circumstances, to reductions of the sentences. Because of their youth, previous clear records or short duration of service, terms were reduced to eight years for 5 men, ten for 11 men, and twelve for 24 men.

The Negro press and other civilian organizations aiding and investigating the case took exceptions to the mutiny charges. It was contended that officers of two of the three divisions to which the men were .attached did not give direct and explicit orders that the men return to work; that in one division which received such direct orders there were no recalcitrants.

A prominent Negro attorney, Thurgood Marshall, representing the National Association for the Advancement of Colored Peoples, who was an observer at the trial, stated:

> The men actually didn't know what happened.
> Had they been given a direct order to load

ammunition, and had they refused to obey that order, then the charges would have been legitimate. But they said no direct order to resume loading was issued them. They were asked whether they would load, and they had replied that they were afraid.

They have told me that they were willing to go to jail to get a change of duty, because of their terrific fear of the explosives, but they had no idea that verbal expression of their fear constituted mutiny.

The accused men were ably defended by White naval officers appointed by the court. They sought to establish that under the circumstances the men were in no mental condition to make sound and considered decisions and statements.

Following the announced sentences, efforts were made to have the reviewing body set aside the convictions or reduce the penalties. Mr. Marshall asked for permission to file a brief, and personally appeared before the Navy's Board of Review on April 3, 1945.

On July 13, 1945, the Navy Department, through acting Secretary Ralph A. Bard, announced that it had been determined that the sentences were legal and that the trial had been fair and impartial.

Request was made by Mr. Marshall for permission to file additional briefs, and for the opportunity for personal presentation of the case before Secretary of the Navy James Forrestal.

Petitions and appeals for clemency were sent from many sources including the daily press, the Negro press, interested organizations and Lester Granger—then on loan to the Navy Department from the National Urban League as Special Aide and Advisor to the Secretary of the Navy. In January 1946, it was announced that the convictions had been set aside, and that the men involved were to be restored to active duty on probation, and were then "presumably overseas."

Personnel at the wartime naval magazines, ammunition and supply depots was predominantly Negro; moreover, these stations were dumping grounds for substandard men. Among these were illiterates, malcontents, chronic disciplinary cases, recalcitrants, and those who met the disfavor of administrative heads and officers of other units and bases. In numerous instances, either inadvertently or intentionally, Negro personnel from Class "A" schools were to be found, and these were assigned menial laborious jobs far removed from their training specialties. Much of the work at these depots was of the common-labor, stevedore type, and often extremely dangerous. White personnel, for the most part, held the ratings and performed most of the technical work. Advancements for Negro personnel were extremely slow—in many cases nonexistent—and particularly slow for those service school graduates whose rates and training could not or was not utilized in the base and station complements. It is obvious that these conditions, plus inadequate living conditions and the limited social intercourse of the stations, were conducive to extreme low morale and dangerous tension among the men. It is surprising that there was not considerably more discontent and disorder at these deports.

The Navy soon began to realize that men trained in technical skills, especially those men trained by the Navy, should not be continued in assignments which did not make use of their abilities. It was in the best interest of the service to see that trained men be allowed to make the most of their opportunities.

Following the Port Chicago incident and other similar experiences of lesser magnitude, three pertinent directives were distributed by the Navy's Bureau of Personnel to all

The Results of Segregation and Discrimination

districts, stations, depots and bases, calling for a more effective utilization of Negro military personnel, the elimination of the practice of maintaining predominantly Negro units at naval magazines, ammunition and supply depots, as well as the practice of dumping wholesale lots of substandard Negro personnel at these places. Subsequent compliance with these directives tended to alleviate many of the glaring problems of Negro personnel facing the Navy.

The Guam Disorders

These disorders, tantamount to mutiny and riot, were disturbances in which Negro naval personnel on the Island of Guam claimed they suffered frequent unprovoked annoyances and assaults by White Marines based on the island, beginning the summer of 1944 and reaching a climax with an unsuccessful venture at retaliation by a group of Negro sailors on Christmas night of the same year. Negro personnel considered work conditions untenable, for although this was an active theater of war, only Whites were armed during work hours in danger zones. They also complained of the lack of reasonable promotions and the failure to place class "A" school graduates in fields for which they were trained. Added to these conditions were the numerous instances of violence suffered at the hands of White Marines who objected to the attentions of the native girls in the village of Agana and about the island by Negro personnel of the base.

On July 7, 1945, publication was made of the matter in the States by Walter White, Secretary of the National Association for the Advancement of Colored People, in a surprise radio broadcast. Forty-five Negro Navy men had been convicted by court martial and given stiff sentences ranging from four months to four years for participating in the "uprising."

It was reported that on Christmas Eve, 1944, a group of White Marines had fired on a group of Negro sailors and had run them out of the main town of the island, mainly because of their attention to local Guamanian girls. That same evening a truckload of White Marines invaded the Negro camp, making threats and charging that one of their number had been struck by a stone thrown by a Negro seaman.

Rumor had it also that a Negro sailor had been killed and another shot by a White Marine on Christmas Day. That brought matters to a head, and Christmas night about forty Negro Navy men left the depot without permission in three commandeered military vehicles, presumably to wreak vengeance upon the Marine Corps camp. They were reported upon departure by the Negro master-at-arms, intercepted and apprehended by White Marine Corps Military Police, who found arms and ammunition in the unauthorized vehicles.

Walter White represented the group as counsel at the Guam trials. The charges included "riot" and unlawful possession and use of United States property, and additional lesser offenses. Three men received terms of less than two years, 33 received sentences of two years, the others twenty-six months to four years.

Efforts in behalf of the men were begun at once by numerous organizations in the States, and continued through 1945. Early in January 1946, it was announced by the Navy Department that the 36 men remaining in confinement at that time would be released and cleared.

Many of the men who served the shorter sentences, and others suspected as having participated or fomented the trouble, were scattered in groups to other island bases and branded as undesirables and troublemakers. Some reached Manana Barracks, Oahu, and were placed in companies of stevedores and general service men. All proved worthy of trust, did an

The Results of Segregation and Discrimination

excellent job at this base and were soon restored to full privileges and duty. Many earned changes of duty in keeping with their service training.

Following this fiasco, directives reached Guam that tended to iron out many of the personnel problems that had beset ammunition and supply depots. Negro chaplains and personnel officers were assigned to the base, and no further difficulties of such magnitude were encountered.

The SeaBees Hunger Strike

A two-day hunger strike by a Navy Construction Battalion was staged at Camp Rousseau, Port Heuneme, California, in March 1945, by Negro seamen in mass protest against Jim Crow practices and the lack of promotions. There was no violence and the thousand men involved continued to work during the strike. After the first day, the station commandant ordered them to the chow hall. The men complied with the order, but refused to touch food while there.

Numerous complaints reached the Bureau of Naval Personnel, over a two-month period, aimed mainly at the commander of the unit, Mississippian P. J. McBean. There were charges of unwarranted segregation and discrimination. The charges of segregation included inequalities in food and quarters, and, above all, of continued injustices and wanton discrimination in matters of promotions.

The outfit had served for twenty-one months overseas, and had made an outstanding record at Tulagi and Guadalcanal, which even their allegedly prejudiced commander had praised.

Prior to the strike, the Navy Department had submitted to the National Association for the Advancement of Colored Peoples a denial by Commander McBean, and by the commandant of the base, who had commended McBean for having "an enlightened and fair attitude toward the colored race" and for being "genuinely interested in their welfare." Nevertheless, he was removed from his command; and after a period of rest and rehabilitation the outfit went overseas again.

The SeaBees Discharge Case

On April 5, 1945, the OWI announced that the Secretary of the Navy had approved the decision of the Department's Board of Review that the discharges of 14 of the 15 Negro SeaBees who were discharged as "undesirable by reason of unfitness" or because of inaptitude" be changed to "discharged under honorable conditions."

Thus ended a case that had been agitated by the press and many organizations for over a year, and had aroused an unusual amount of interest on the part of the public. The case grew out of the discharge in October 1943 of 19 men who were members of the 80th SeaBee Battalion. At the time of the discharge no specific grounds for the action were made public, but certain occurrences that had preceded the action were regarded as the cause.

Shortly before the multiple discharge, 12 members of the battalion were urged to air their grievances concerning race conditions at the base. These men later testified that they were encouraged to talk "straight from the shoulder" in the presence of their commanding officer, and were also told the meeting was off the record. Thus assured, they did not hesitate to state their views on conditions they felt were discriminatory, particularly the battalion's promotion policy.

Eighty percent of the battalion was Negro, they pointed out, yet none were rated above petty officer, second class, whereas the remaining 20 percent—the White personnel—were without exception rated higher in rank.

The Results of Segregation and Discrimination

The commanding officer promised further meetings on the subject and the formation of a committee on race matters, to be organized by the chaplain. But on the day following, the commanding officer called the men together, dressed them down for "griping" and announced there would be no more meetings. A few days later the 12 men and 7 others not present at the original conference were discharged. Of these 19 men, 16 were discharged as "undesirables" and 3 for "unfitness and inaptitude." The latter men were eventually given "honorable" discharges.

There was much protest when the case became known to the public. The matter was taken to Secretary Knox, who decided that there were no grounds for relief. An appeal for reconsideration met no favor. The efforts and agitation of many organizations continued.

In June 1944, the Bill of Rights for Servicemen had been made law by Congress. A provision in the law stated that persons discharged from the armed forces could have their discharges reviewed by a reviewing board. Fifteen of the 16 men discharged as "undesirable" joined in a petition for the review of their cases.

The review was granted and a hearing set for December 1944. Fourteen of the 15 men were given discharges that stated "under honorable conditions." One petitioner was refused because of a bad record prior to the incident preceding his discharge.

The announcement of the decision of the reviewing body in the case of the 16 Seabees in April 1945, and the Seabee's hunger strike in March of the same year stimulated the Navy Department to clarify its policies. The Directive of June 1945 was sent to all commanding officers handling Negro personnel.

> *Directive (CNO) June 1945*
> Negro Enlisted Personnel—Expanded Assignment of to Commands and Activities in the Pacific Ocean Area
> In order that there by a uniform interpretation of the policy of the Navy Department in regard to the utilization of Negro personnel, it may be helpful to point out that it is the Navy's policy to:
> 1. Assign and utilize Negro personnel on exactly the same basis as White personnel, in the same type of work.
> 2. Assure that Negroes are given the same opportunity as Whites to qualify for all rates and rating branches.
> 3. Assure that Negroes are afforded the same opportunity for advancement in pay grades on the same basis as Whites, in accordance with existing regulations.
> 4. Avoid the issuance of orders, or use of signs, restricting the use of facilities such as "heads," Ship's Service, sleeping quarters, mess, etc., to one or the other of the races.

And so by the costly process of trial and error and hit and miss, the headaches of segregation gradually began to give way to total integration.

For many years the Navy listed racial groups according to general or specific nationalities, such as:

Puerto Rican (Negro)
Puerto Rican (White)
Chinese

The Results of Segregation and Discrimination

Japanese
Korean
American Indian
Negro
Filipino
Samoan
Chamorro
Hawaiian

By order of the Personnel Policy Board of the Secretary of Defense (April 5, 1950) all racial entries and designators in records and forms of the armed forces were to be incorporated in the following categories:

a. Caucasian   White
      Puerto Rican (White)
b. Negroid   Negro
      Puerto Rican (Negro)
c. Mongolian   Chinese
      Japanese
      Korean
d. Indian   American Indian
e. Malayan   Filipino
      Samoan
      Chamorro
      Hawaii

The question arises, what is "race?" UNESCO stated that "A race is any group of people whom others choose to describe as a 'race.'" In drawing up the above classification, the Office of the Secretary of Defense has stepped in where ethnologists fear to tread. The classification is arbitrary and tends to fit the man to the pattern. It is generally accepted that there are but three ethnic groups of man: Mongoloids, Negroids and Caucasians. The American Indians are not a race per se but are true Mongoloids. The word "Negroid," as listed, is objectionable, and the category "Puerto Rican (Negro)" is not a scientific determination but a misconception, pure and simple. In New York City, Puerto Ricans have in some instances refused to enlist because of this situation. Puerto Ricans are being enlisted as "Caucasian" or "Negroid" depending on skin color or admission of the prospective recruit. One instance stands out where two brothers—one dark and the other fair—were enlisted according to the official classification. When it was discovered the two men were brothers, the fair one was then listed as "Negroid"—and he immediately terminated his enlistment.

Racial designators could well be entirely eliminated, and experience has shown that such elimination would be preferable to the unintelligible manner in which such matters are now handled. The Navy no longer classifies race except on medical forms. In 1949 Judge Charles Fahy, Chairman of the President's Committee on Equality of Treatment and Opportunity in the Armed Services, sent this letter to Louis Johnson, at that time Secretary of Defense:

30 November 1949

Dear Mr. Secretary:
It has been brought to my attention that the Chairman of the Personnel Policy Board has approved a policy directing that whenever entries regarding race are required on enlistment records and shipping articles, recruits shall be identified in the following racial categories:

The Results of Segregation and Discrimination

1. Caucasian
2. Negroid
3. Mongolian
4. Indian (American)
5. Malayan

I understand that the Chairman of the Personnel Policy Board has ordered the three Service Secretaries to place this policy into effect as soon as practicable.

While I can see no positive harm in this policy, it seems to me that it unnecessarily multiplies racial distinctions at a time when the whole trend is to get away from emphasis on race. As you know, the Navy now indicates race only on its medical records, and the Army and Air Force employ only two racial categories—White and Negro.

Furthermore, this multiplication of racial categories, it seems to me, is capable of causing much confusion and may result in misunderstanding which could be unpleasant and troublesome. Even anthropologists are not in complete agreement on racial categories, and I think it is asking a good deal of a recruiting sergeant that he be called upon to classify recruits into five distinct groups when it is often impossible so to classify them because of a mixture of racial and national antecedents.

I realize that it is advantageous to have personnel classifications uniform in the three services, but I did want to indicate to you my doubts about the wisdom of increasing racial distinctions.

Charles Fahy
Chairman

The Navy took the initial and most far-reaching steps toward integration and the elimination of such racial classifications. The United Nations, the State Department, UNESCO, Selective Service and civilian agencies and organizations worked toward and achieved the same objectives.

Those of us who pioneered in the Navy during World War II aided in bringing about this initial stage of total integration in the military. The author was a witness of this great effort in 1945 while he was on duty at Great Lakes. It was a wonderful revelation viewing Black and White recruits training together.

CHAPTER 3

THE SAGA OF BLACK NAVY VETERANS OF WORLD WAR II: AN AMERICAN TRIUMPH

In his book *We are Men,* Wilbert L. Walker talks about his experience of discrimination. As a young Black man from Baltimore he entered the Navy during World War II. He was willing to do his share in that great fight to preserve democracy against the fascist force of Germany, Italy and Japan. Instead, he found himself fully embattled against bigotry, segregation and other undemocratic customs practiced by White Americans.

This experience in the Navy was shared by thousands of Black men and women during World War II. Indeed, segregation and discrimination was practiced widely in military and civilian life. Despite these barriers, we were willing to do our part to defeat the enemies of democracy. Much of my energy, however, was devoted to fighting the undemocratic practices of segregation and discrimination.

The Author's War Experience

My experiences were similar to those of Wilber Walker's and other Black sailors in the United States Navy during World War, II. It was a very humiliating experience to be segregated and discriminated against while serving in the military and laying your life on the line to make the world safe for democracy. Then, too, one had to volunteer for the Navy in order to get in. I left West Hartford, Connecticut and was inducted into the Navy September 12th, 1942 in Baltimore,

Maryland. I was promised the petty officer's rating of "Welfare Worker," assistant to the chaplain but was denied the rating once I arrived at Great Lakes. When I applied for the rating the personnel officer told me that I could not get it because I could not play the organ. Nowhere did the published requirements for the rating mention playing the organ a requirement. I had more than the published requirements; a B.S. degree from Southern University; an M.A. degree in religious education with a psychology major from Hartford Seminary. I had taught high school in Natchotoches, Louisiana for one and a half years; and worked as a social group worker for over a year. This was my second direct experience of discrimination in the Navy. The first was being placed in the all-Negro Camp Robert Smalls at Great Lakes as a member of Company 924. Our company commander was Chief Petty Officer Wolf, White.

    I was made apprentice chief petty officer of my company by commander Wolf and felt good about it. To me, a non-military minded person, this experience was good for it aided me in the development of a positive attitude toward the Navy in spite of being in a segregated unit. Another bit of humiliation educated Black recruits faced was denial of ratings and ranks leading to non-commission and commission officers. Many of the Negro naval recruits were college and university graduates but they were not afforded the opportunity to be commissioned officers. It was also difficult for them to become non-commissioned officers.

    I was fortunate enough to be selected to attend one of the "grade A" service schools conducted at Great Lakes. It was the school of navigation which trained recruits who qualified, after passing the Navy's stiff classification test, to become quartermasters and signalmen aboard ships at sea. Only ten percent of the graduates of the course could be rated petty officer third class. Again, I was lucky enough to receive a high enough grade to be rated quartermaster third class (QM 3/C) upon graduation.

Upon graduation from service school I was one of the few graduates that received a petty officer's rating of Quarter Master Third Class (QM 3/C). Only about ten percent of the class was rated; the others were sent away as strikers for the ratings of Quartermaster or Signalman.

A strange thing happened on my way to sea after graduation. My mother, Ardell Peters, who was living in Berkeley, California came for my graduation in order to be with me prior to my "putting to sea." Before leaving the base for liberty in Chicago with my mother I received orders to report to the personnel office "on the double." This I did and received the best of news. As luck would have it, orders had come to Great Lakes from the Bureau of Navy Personnel, Washington, D.C., for me to remain at Great Lakes and supervise the Remedial Education Program of Camp Robert Smalls and the other camps that were being opened for Negroes. They were Camps Moffett and Lawrence. My rating was changed to that of Specialist Teacher, Third Class (SPT 3/C) Petty Officer. I reorganized the program, selected college graduates to teach, and set the stage for establishment of "The Special Training Unit," a day school program for educationally deficient Navy recruits.

My mother and I stayed in Chicago a few days visiting old friends from home Monroe, Baton Rouge, and New Orleans, Louisiana. We stayed with Mrs. Robert Perkins and her son Robert. On that Sunday we visited the C.M.E. (Community Methodist Church) where we were well received. Mrs. Charlotte Greenough made us welcome in her home and invited me to make it my home when in Chicago. This I did throughout my tenure of over three years at Great Lakes. Her daughters,

Billie and Evelyn treated me like their brother. Billie's son, Johnny Griffin became a world renowned saxophone player.

My wife Marie was ecstatic over the good news. Right then and there she made preparation to come to Great Lakes for Christmas holidays of 1942. Through friends that I made in Chicago I was instrumental in getting a nice place for her to stay in Waukegan, Illinois with a fine Negro family, Dr. and Mrs. Robert G. Smith. They had a daughter Francis who was a sophomore at the University of Wisconsin in Madison. We had a lovely time with the Smiths, the leading Negro family in the area. They had a lovely house in the suburban area and they opened it up to other Black sailors from Great Lakes. North Chicago and Waugkegan were "Jim Crow" towns and very discriminating. The Negro sailors could go to one club in Waugkegan—"Club Afrik." The other clubs and places of amusement were off limits to us. We had to go to Chicago, Milwaukee and Gary, Indiana for recreation. We had loads of fun with the Smiths, their friends, other sailors and their wives during the holidays of 1942.

The next year, after much study, The Bureau of Naval Personnel decided that more manpower was needed so standards were lowered so that non-high school graduates could volunteer and enter the Navy if they met physical and mental criteria. Because I was a psychologist-teacher I was assigned to administer psychological and educational tests to the Negro recruits entering the Navy at Great Lakes Naval Training Center with my two assistants, David Steele and Henry Chaney. Individuals who did not meet the mental level (I.Q.) were surveyed out of the Navy immediately. Those who failed the education tests and passed the mental tests were placed in the newly established special training unit. They were kept in the unit for sixteen weeks and were taught by the unit's teachers. Once they reached a high school equivalence level they were graduated and sent, on a whole, to ammunition bases in the united States. Some went out to sea around the coasts as strikers for their rating.

When the Special Training Unit was established in 1943, I was relieved of duties as superintendent of the remedial education school which was created under auspices of Chaplain Flower's Office which was under the command of D. W. Armstrong. Three well-educated recruits, William Thomas, Lewis Williams and Reginald Goodwin had recommended to Commander Armstrong that a system of off duty education be provided recruits that failed the Navy classification test that they administered and scored. I was selected by Commander Armstrong after I told him how I felt discriminated against after volunteering for the Navy. My first encounter with Commander Armstrong was shortly after I arrived at Great Lakes, September 12, 1942, for recruit training at Camp Robert Smalls. Upon inquiring about the Specialist rating of Welfare Worker, Assistant to the Chaplain, that I had signed up for when I was inducted into the service I was informed that I could not have it because I could not play an organ. I was furious for I met all of the published requirements for the rating and was recommended for it.

Well, I decided to go directly to Commander Armstrong and protest this blatant act of discrimination. I went to his office early one morning without an appointment. When he heard my story, and that I was concerned about the morale of the Negro sailor, he said, "By God, Peters! That is what I am concerned about; the morale of the Negro sailor!" He sent me to see Chaplain Flowers, White, a wonderful old fashioned Southern Baptist Preacher from Georgia who had a heart of gold. Under his supervision a remedial education program had been started by William Thomas, Lewis Williams and Reginald Goodwin. They welcomed me with open arms, and because of their busy schedule in the classification office, I was put in charge of this off duty evening education program while in recruit training and, later, attending Quarter Master (Navigation) service school during the day.

The Special Training Unit had to have a commissioned officer in charge. The initial administrator was one of the first Negro commissioned Officers, Ensign Reginald Goodwin; the second, a Negro, Ensign Dennis Nelson; the third, White, Lieutenant Lynn. I was made psychologist for the unit with special duties in the Neuropsychiatric Unit under its chief psychologist, Dr. S. B. Cummings. My duties involved testing, evaluation and research. Truly, my experience in both units set the course for my later professional life. The White psychologists and psychiatrists were wonderful to me. They felt that I should be a commissioned officer with the rank of Lieutenant junior grade; skipping over that of ensign as they had done. They recommended that I be given the Navy Officer's Qualifying Test which I passed with flying colors. Well, the rest follows:

The Chief Psychologist of the Bureau of Naval Personnel, Dr. William Hunt, came to Great Lakes to interview me regarding a commission in the Navy as a psychologist for which I had qualified. He asked me a number of questions about psychology, academic and cultural background, which I answered to the best of my ability. After this line of questioning he inquired if I had a Ph.D. I told him no but that I had a M.A. degree in psychology. He replied that although they were commissioning White men and women with bachelor and master degrees in psychology he felt that future commissions in psychology should only go to those with Ph.D.s. He left and promised me that I would be hearing from him. About two or three months later a speed letter came informing me that "at the present time there was no billet available for one with my qualifications, and that at a latter date I would be commissioned."

This was a real blow to me. The officers that I worked with in the Neuropsychiatric Unit were disappointed for they knew of my work and had recommended me for the commission. They had even suggested that I go in to Chicago and purchase my uniform for I had passed the Navy Officer Qualifying test and, seemingly the interview, but I refused to do so. They told me, which I knew, that my being denied a commission was rank discrimination. They even asked if I wanted out of the Navy; if so they could recommend a "situation discharge" based on psychological stress. I thanked them and said no, that I wanted to carry on for my work was too important and rewarding.

In late 1943 or early 1944 two additional camps for Negroes were opened at Great Lakes; Camp Lawrence and Camp Moffett. This made added psychological work for my team members and me because many of the new recruits were selected for the Special Training unit. I was busier than a "one armed paper hanger" during that period, but not busy enough for the deputy supervisor of the unit, Chief Petty Officer Mareno, a former probation officer from San Francisco. For some reason that I could never understand he took a strong dislike to me and constantly threatened to send me to the "outgoing unit" for duty at sea. I finally got fed up with his "bullshit" and decided to take my case to Commander Armstrong.

I made an appointment to see Commander Armstrong through his yeoman. He gave me the appointment immediately when I informed him that it was urgent. I arrived at his office with a box filled with psychological and education work that I had done for the Special Training and Neuropsychiatric Units. I placed it on his desk and requested that he examine it to determine its importance. He responded after the examination that it was damn important; a real contribution to his command at Great Lakes and the war effort of the Department of the Navy. Following that retort I told him that Chief Petty Officer Mareno said that the work was unimportant and was harassing me, therefore, I wanted to be relieved of my duties and sent away from Great Lakes for he was threatening to send me to sea.

After hearing me out Commander Armstrong said that Mareno was a fool if he thought that my work was not important; he had no business being a part of an educational unit. He called his yeoman and told him to get Mareno on the phone immediately. When Moreno got on the phone he told him to pack gear "sea going fashion" and report to the Out Going Unit for shipment to the South Pacific command. This was the last I saw or heard of Chief Mareno. I remained at Great Lakes for my full tour of duty with the United States Navy during World War II.

In May 1945, I went to sleep in my bunk at Camp Robert Smalls and awoke to the sound of recruits marching to the beat of a drum and singing. I looked out of my window and saw that my dream and efforts in the U.S. Navy at Great Lakes had been realized. In the unit of sailors that were passing was a mixture of White and Negro recruits. On that day the other units were mixed and the three separate camps for Negroes had been disbanded. Total integration had come to Great Lakes and perhaps, to the rest of the U.S. Navy.

The following accounts were recorded at the World War II Black Navy Veterans of Great Lakes celebration of the 50th anniversary of admission of African-Americans into the general service of the United States Navy, June 20th, 1992.

An American Triumph

Dr. Charles Yepan, Jr.

"My name is Dr. Charles Yepan, Jr. Chicago is my home now. I was born in New Orleans, Louisiana and I went to high school in Vicksburgh, Mississippi and under the Navy I enjoyed a good time, in fact I got my schooling there. I became an optometrist through the educational program that they gave and if it wasn't for the Navy maybe I wouldn't have made this deal so I'm grateful to the Navy. I went in in 1943 on July the 11th and I came out in 1946 in January 11 and I was in the shore patrol and I served 16 months Chicago, 6 in Detroit and 6 in Milwaukee. I was a little disappointed at first because I qualified for a job like aviation metal smith. I had a three point six average and I felt I should have gotten it, or something better, but times changed and I went along with the times and I'm glad to see the progress that's being made now. I was denied that position because I was African-American. In those days, the Navy was like all the government, pretty segregated, but there's been great change. Especially with the advent of Dr. King there's been quite a change."

Jesse Arbor

"My name is Jesse Arbor. I enlisted in the Navy from Chicago September 11, 1942. I was from Chicago. I was in the 9th company the 922. When I started off I was 321 and I was in about the 3rd or 4th company that was formed in 1942. I must say if there was any one thing that impacted on me more than anything was the fact that they saved me from having to go into the Army. I don't know what would have happened to me if I went into the Army because I had three brothers already in the Army. One for four years and I didn't know the difference between either one of them. And they told me if I got to try any place to go any place other than this man's Army don't come in. Well all of us were into Army, Navy and there wasn't no such thing as Navy because I tried to join the Army or than Navy when I got out of high school in 1929. So I went on to college for three and a half years and when my money ran out—my football eligibility, that's when I went on the road and came here. I was 26 when I went in to the Navy. As a matter of fact, practically all of us who went in the first group of commission officers were too old for the rank they gave us. We went in as ensigns and some of them were too old for commanders, but when they commissioned us they didn't know what they wanted to do with us, so the bad part about it all our chief petty officers, at that time were high school grads and college grads. All the Black troops came in as enlisted men so part of the golden thirteen were officers in their thirties; too old to be ensigns so they automatically had to jump them up to their age bracket. So some jumped from chief to lieutenant commanders after they commissioned us because we were just blanketed in as ensigns whether we were eighteen or eighty. It impacted not only the Black sailor, but the White sailor who was in there. Because they couldn't afford to let us come in with the same rank as our instructors. It was so ramified until it's really pathetic to look back in retrospect, but I think we were level headed and took things in stride as the old adage goes. If someone bears you a lemon, go and make lemonade out of it. That's exactly what we did."

Reverend Rudy Jackson

"My name is Reverend Rudy Jackson. I went into the service in November 1942. I was one of the first groups that went into Robert Smalls. I was Company 1752 and we went in there and that was the first time we found out we were segregated in a separate camp. It didn't effect us that much because we knew we were on the ball. I had come out of the

ROTC in high school. When I got there I informed the chief and he said, "Well, we will make you the apprentice CPO of the company." I became the apprentice CPO and in the course of being the apprentice CPO, I put forth all of the good efforts I had from the ROTC. In fact I formed the first rifle team that did a special drill at Camp Robert Smalls in November of 1942. It was twelve of us and we practiced and we perfected. We were using 1903 rifles. They were very heavy."

I was shipped to school. I went to machinist school at Hampton Institute, after being there we met an instructor and he told us, he said, "You have been sent to a segregated school, but you will come out of here the best." And we studied hard and in the course of between school and Great Lakes I asked the officer if I could go to OCS. He informed me that I had to have two years of college. We had previously known that the Whites were coming out of high school and being sent to OCS, and they had a fellow that was a drop out and had gone to OCS; we knew this but we couldn't do anything about it. I went to school I learned diesel engines and lathe and drill presses and when I left school I was shipped to New Jersey."

I stayed in New Jersey about a month. During that time I worked in a machine shop and we were cutting rods for ships. These were precision cutting in cutting threads on these rods. These were precision tools that we were dealing with and we had to have so many within a few days and we succeeded in doing that. Even in New Jersey, we were in a separate barracks. They refused to integrate the barracks there. Then I left there and went to New York. I stayed in New York for one day. That was the one place that was not segregated. We were stationed in a hotel on Long Island. We stayed there one week. That was where they even had officers serving the tables in the chow hall and I stayed there. They gave me one liberty. When I came back off of liberty I met one of the commanders coming in the door and he said, "Jackson, you are being transferred to California. I went to Shoemaker, California and that was where they had a riot. Now this was not in the news. But they had a riot there because they had segregated lines in the chow hall and I have to say it like it happened. One of the White fellows came up and told us, "Nigger, get out of the line." And one of the fellows hit him and this started the fight; it went into the chow hall. It tore up the chow hall. Then they restricted us to the barracks. They shipped us out a couple of days later. I went to Hawaii to Adwitock and from Adwitock to Quaduline and from Quaduline to Guam."

I spent all of my time in the Pacific. On Guam, even, we were separated. We were back in the jungle and we had built our camp from the ground up. We built a tennis court, we built our own movie theater, we did everything ourselves, and after I was there for a while we were working on what they call revetments. This was loading and unloading ammunition, very dangerous, very highly explosive and we did this for a while, and then when the war was over and Japan had surrendered they started shipping us home on the point system. Before my points were up, there were two pharmacists there who I got to be buddies with they were shipping out and the doctor asked them, "Who can we make to take your place in the camp?" And they said me, now I was a fireman, I was a machinist mate. And the doctor says, "Can you learn this?" I said, "Yes." And inside of three weeks they taught me quite a bit about medicine. They left and I came home in February 1946. It was quite a day for me."

When I got back to Chicago, I was completely turned around, I didn't know north from south, east from west and I caught a cab to get home, and when I got home the smallest thing I had was a fifty and the cab driver told me, "It's on me, I'm glad to see you back." My mother and father had kept the

Christmas tree up for all the boys to see after getting back home."

Interviewer: "The ones that gave you an opportunity with the medicine, the pharmacists, whatever, now were they Black?"

"Yes they were; the whole camp was Black. There was no Whites there at all, in fact, when they were getting ready to take us out and send us home they were having a bunch of fellows down at the main base they were going to bring up to our camp. When we found out they were all White we told them, "You bring them up, we will tear the camp up." Because if they cannot come here and work for this, then they cannot enjoy."

Interviewer: "Did you go to Chicago to high school?"

"Yes, I went to Desable High School for the ROTC. In fact, I ended up on the city staff.

Interviewer: "Was it a Black high school?"

"Yes, an all Black high school; in fact, there were only two at that time, Wendell Phillips and DeSable. Those were the only high schools in Chicago that Blacks went to."

Interviewer: "Because you did have ROTC; who taught you ROTC if Blacks had not been in?"

"It was a White sergeant, I can't think of his name, but he was good. Well in the second year of ROTC I won the gold tribune metal that was a high honor and you won metals in different things in the ROTC."

Interviewer: "When did you become a minister? In 1950?"

"Yes! I have been in the ministry for quite some time. I've gone to different schools; Chicago Baptist Institute, Chicago Teachers College Metropolitan School of Music, and American College of Music. I've studied and have found that studying is the best thing for anyone to do. I like to work with youngsters and I try to encourage them to always study; make yourself, you have a brain—use it. Because when you use your brain then you have accomplished something. And you leave something for somebody else."

Wyman Vaughns

"My name is Wyman Vaughns and I entered the Navy in Camp Robert Smalls in September 9, 1942 and from there I made service school at Hampton Institute, Hampton, Virginia. I attended electricians mate school. While at Hampton I spoke to commemorate the Black man for going to all branches of the Navy. I spoke on mutual network then nationwide. I spoke for the Navy and an Army guy for the Army. He was at Hampton at the same time. While at Hampton I was made electrician's mate. I finished there and was sent to Newport, Rhode Island. While at Newport for about three months Captain Downs came to check on the Black sailors. When we went there he asked me directly what was I doing. I told him that I had been here three months and I'm not with the machine shop; I'm over at the barracks."

Three months after he left that was changed. I was put in the machine shop because I was an electrician second class so from there I made, also, another service school. I went to Brooklyn, New York. After that I came out of there and they brought me in and shipped me overseas. Before going over seas though I went to a place called Shoemaker; that's where all the guys go to be shipped overseas on ships. There was a big war on then, the war was very plentiful. They were looking for somebody to operate the movies. Well since I went to technician school they found me and the guy called in and he said 'do you know that out of all these thousand men here you're the only one that's actually capable to operate the movie projector?' And so that kept me from going over seas and they sent me to one of the barracks and

An American Triumph

I went there and that's where we used to repair them and what have you from the big ships that's coming in and we serviced them with movies and all what have you and eventually our captain came through and he bounced me and I went in the service over seas."

We stopped at a place called Attaweetah where we had a beer outings because we were going a long, long way. While we were there we woke up the next morning and the ship was weaving and bobbing; at the time that we were at Attaweetah a one man sub hit our sister ship and blew it up; hit the Magazine and we didn't know anything about it until we got way off at sea because when you're on board a ship that's just like being in a vault, you don't hear nothing."

We went on in and after we got so far in we ended up at Cavite, fifty miles from Manila. I was shipped from there. The magic thing about it was before we got settled I had seven White guys with me and I was ahead of them, but we stayed out on that duty from island to island so long that the ship was having to use a mitchem to take us from one place to another."

One day we were in the barracks and Slim, we used to call him Slim; he was from Philadelphia, and he said, 'Fellows do you know how long we've been going off on these islands and what have you?' I said, 'Man, about two months.' He said, 'I wonder why?' And Slim said, 'You know why? Because what's Wyman's rate?' 'Well, he's a second class electrician mate.' He said, 'Well, they don't know what to do with him.' And that was true. The only thing they could put me on was a sea going tug. That's the smallest thing they could think of putting me on was a sea going tug. So due to that I just had a feast, it was nice so I didn't mind. They didn't want me to fight, well, gee! Then from there that's when we came from Cavite; fifty miles from Manila and that was the short ending of my experiences."

The Saga of Black Navy Veterans of World War II

Milburn Cananzie

"My name is Milburn Cananzie and I joined the Navy in 1963 while I was a junior at Dunbar Vocational High School here in Chicago and I retired December 1989 with two years active duty, 24 years reserve."

Interviewer: "What do you think of these World War II Veterans?"

"They have some delightful stories and I don't want to concentrate on the negative aspects, but the positive contributions that these few gentlemen stuck together to preserve their story so that it could become a part of history; a part that needs to be told during the hardships that they lived under, they were able to endure and still serve our country with distinction. To me that's what makes it great that they're here, not embittered about anything but just here in an atmosphere of celebration to say, 'Hey, we endured.' They're proud of what they did."

I had a somewhat similar experience like this in 1965. I was up in Quincy Point, Rhode Island and it was during the time Dr. King had his marches and the papers were full of pictures about let's say the height of the civil rights movement and this experience where he was featured in a magazine and someone had taken the magazine and scratched out King and put Coon there and just hung it up in a naval office. I remember when I got there Monday morning and saw it and I took it to my commanding officer which I now consider a pretty bold move on my part, but the way my commanding officer reacted was really a bold move on his part because he took the paper from me and the next morning he called an All Hands Muster and held it up and said I will have none of this in my squadron. I recall this is in 1965 before equal opportunity in the Navy was even thought about and he just told anyone who's got a problem with Blacks or Negroes being in the Navy were to get out of his Navy and my respect for that Commander Dorn was just overwhelmed by him taking this positive step to say to everyone there, because there was only about four minorities in a squadron of about 350 men, and he said 'anybody got a problem with this, get out of my Navy.'"

Interviewer: "What do you think of the *esprit de corps* of these men?"

"Oh, the camaraderie we need that, the networking, the supporting that these men have; because I was at a meeting earlier today, I'm a volunteer in the school system and it was why can't Black men get together and support our Black views in numbers; why are we so standoffish from one another? And to see this type of camaraderie; I have admiration for support groups like this because as we know the women have it all the time; they've got all kinds of sisterhoods, but when it comes to men we don't have any brotherhoods, so to see this is really admirable."

December 1989 I thought it was all over with and I got a call in March of 1990 from my commanding officer saying 'put your uniform back on as if you have never retired; you've been awarded the Navy achievement metal' and he says 'and I want to pin that on you.' For achievement metal is really a reservist to be awarded the Navy achievement unique occurrence; because they're normally 95% of the time awarded to active duty people."

Charles J. Williams

"My name is Charles J. Williams and I was in Camp Robert Smalls December 4, 1942 and went through the basic training there and some of the things that we saw that went on in Robert Smalls was something that you never will forget. Tonight as I look at these admirals and these commanders and whatnot tears come to my eyes. Being in this organization with Dr. Peters, one of the founders, and Jim Howard to get this organization started like this and for us to bring out the history that our American people; not only Blacks but Whites have missed out on this is one of the things that we really do; go around and speak to the people about our part of the history; that we have served in the Navy. Now we are beginning to get around to having told a little bit more and we go around to the schools speaking about their education and their history."

We had to come the hard, hard way, but the fruit of our work is when we see Admiral Gravery, Admiral Gaston and other people like that that have come over our backs to make this Navy a better Navy than what it was in 1941 and 1942. Our heroes Dorie Miller, Jessie L. Brown are just about forgotten, and the American people should wake up and realize that some of these people are still living. Bataan survivors and all those people that were the ones that fought and stood up for our protection and we should not forget them as long as we live."

So that's why I'm happy to be with the Navy veterans because we stand up for a cause and we're looking for a better situation, a better world. That way we will help the whole nation."

Leroy Colston

"My name is Leroy Colston, the President of the Chicago Chapter, World War II Black Navy Veterans. I went in the United States Navy at a very young age. It was June eighteen, 1943. I got my training at Camp Robert Smalls. And from there I came out of Camp Robert Smalls boot camp and went into security watch and I stayed in security watch for about three or four months and from there I went to Corpus Christi, Texas."

"I was among the first hundred and one Black men to go to Corpus Christi, Texas Navy Air Station. I worked A&R, which is an air craft carrier machine shop or something. It was a job which I did not think that I should do in the Navy, so I took it upon myself and went to the Welfare Department and asked for something to do a little different. At which time they gave me a job as an M.A. (Master of Arms) and I put together a plan and we had two separate recreation areas; one was known North Gate which was White and South Gate which was Black. I promoted entertainment for the South Gate which we conducted amateur hours, happy hours and other forms of entertainment."

After that, an order came down to desegregate the buses which were on the base where the Black men rode in the back of the bus. I was given a job integrating the buses on the Navy air station; this was in the year 1944, as a matter of fact the last of '44 and the first of '45. I would ride the bus and make sure the Black men were not bothered when they sat anywhere on the bus that they wanted. The Whites got used to seeing them riding all over the bus."

After that was over I had tour in the South Pacific. I went to Allaweetah, the Marshall Islands, after going to the Marshall Islands we sat out there and drank by the ocean on APL (advanced personnel lodging). I was affiliated with the 52nd Marine Defense and we were called the Logistics Support Men. And we sat there for nine months and my company worked ship to ship doing stevedore work. I caught some of the small SCMs from boat to boat; boat to boat; boat to boat."

After that I went to Guam and from Guam I came back to the states in 1946. From there I was discharged out at Great Lakes. It was a wonderful experience, I wouldn't trade it for anything in the world."

Fred Ross

"I am Fred Ross. I attended Dillard University in New Orleans. There were 66 of us who left the scholars. We were there when Tora came in. I was a ROTC officer, so I had to leave."

I called my mother long distance and came back to Chicago and I went downtown to the post office where the marine corps was and they said they weren't ready for me. I said very good so I went to the Navy department and they told me to get myself in order and get on a train and go to Great Lakes, and I did so. When I got there they said, 'Are you an ROTC officer?' I said,'Yes, in high school.' They said, 'What high school?' I said, 'Sergeant Hen High. I was assistant PMS&T.' He said, 'All right, Mr. Ross, I understand you went to Fort Riley Camp.' I said, 'Yes, I was sent up there from Chicago to learn PO tags and so forth.' He said, 'You think you're ready?' I said, 'I'm ready.' So they put me on a train and sent me to Great Lakes."

I got there in the evening and reported to the headquarters building and I ran into a gentlemen from the University of Minnesota; I ran track against him at Chicago State when I was in high school. He was going to be my company commander so when he saw me he came over and said, 'Fred Ross?' I said, 'Yup, that's right.' He said, 'You're in my company.' And that's when the ballgame started. So I worked with him in three companies and then I became a company commander and trained six companies of my own."

When I got through with that, I got there on October the 27th and I came out of the Navy, that was November the 5th at 9:50 in the morning. They asked me to come back as a warrant officer and my mother said, 'No way; he's going to college.' So I came home and I started going to school. I went to DePaul University; no there was another school there before that, but DePaul was my target, I went there and I took a degree in Philosophy, and when I got through with that; I started teaching. I took a teacher's exam. I took a police exam;

my wife didn't like it. She didn't want me to be an officer, she didn't want me to be a fireman. I said, 'Very well, I'll get a job at the post office so I can maintain the household and I will go to DePaul and get my degree.' And I did that."

And now we have four children. My oldest child is a daughter, she has her masters and she's teaching and she's working on a Ph.D. My son is a psychologist. He graduated from high school and I sent him to Cornell so he wouldn't have to go overseas. I learned that game fast. And then when he came out I sent him to Talidega to become a chemist. He's now a psychologist and he's married. Then I have two daughters. My youngest daughter is a gynecologist, an obstetrical person. She finally got married and we have a granddaughter. And this worked out very well."

Crackton Hill

"My name is Crackton Hill. World War II Black Navy Veteran's Company 922 and in '43 they shipped me out to Hampton Institute for motor machinist and diesel and gasoline. I was there for four months. Upon graduation they sent Gravely and myself to San Diego, Point Loma. Before we left, Admiral Gravely, he's an Admiral now, but he was just a plain recruit, like myself, but Lt. Commander Downs, who was our commander, could only give so many third and second class ratings. So he gave me a letter. He said, 'When you get to your base, give the commanding officer there this letter and he will give you your petty officer rating, third class.'"

When I got to the base, Point Loma, I gave it to the commanding officer, and he told me no Negro would get a rating under him. Commander Downs was going around from base to base checking on integration with the Blacks and the Whites. So, he came out to the base and had inspection and the troops, Gravely and myself were in line and we were standing side by side. Gravely was the first one Lt. Commander Downs asked to step forward, which he did. He looked and he had his second class petty officer rating on, Then he told him how I was being treated and everything. Then he asked me to step forward and I still had my red stripe around my arm so he asked me he said, 'Hill, where's your rating?' Not thinking, he caught me off guard. I said, 'Lt. Commander Nabastagget told me no Negro would get a rating under him.' He said, 'What? Repeat that.' Now I'm there with my officer at the base, I had to repeat it, so I said 'Commander Nabastagget told me no Negro would get a rating under him.' He said, 'Okay, step back.' And Lt. Nabastagget turned red as a tomato because this was a Lt. Commander and his brother was an admiral in the Navy with the fleet so he had weight."

The next week he gave me my rating and kicked me off the base and sent me into San Diego to shore patrol so when I got in there I reported to the commander and I told him what happened. So he said, 'Well, Hill, you are the first Black S.P. of the Navy' and that was in '43 and right after that we had the zoot suit riot from Frisco all the way up the coast line into San Diego and I was involved in the whole shebang for I would say about three months. And then after that I was the Sr. Shore Patrol there. Then they set up a shore patrol at Great Lakes and as they were graduating and coming out to the west coast I instructed them in the duties that were happening on the west coast."

After that they put me on riding the San Diego train from San Diego to L.A. A layover in L.A.; take a train out of there to Albuquerque, New Mexico. From there we would come back to San Diego. After that, they had a hunger strike at Port Hueneme, California. By me being the Senior Shore Patrol they sent me there for duties as shore patrol. They had this hunger strike and I had to take convoys into Watts to pick up rations for the company. The riot in Watts was later. I was in Watts when trouble was brewing there. That was in '44 or '45 because they had built a road because we were beginning to get C.B.s (construction battalion). They had just made it a construction battalion thing and then they wanted to ship me to Hawaii and I refused; then they wanted to ship me to the Philippines and I refused; but in those days I'll say it was a political thing and I was in charge with the activities of the base such as gambling and what have you and I was making a nice buck."

At Port Hueneme they were going to ship me over to Tokyo, Japan, and I didn't want to go. I refused to go and then I checked with the yeoman and found out I was a half a point short before I could muster myself out. I told the commander, you see we weren't flying we were going by ship, so I told him, 'Now I'll tell you as soon as the boat lands in Japan I'm going to get off and get right back on the boat and come back to the states because I'll have my points.'"

So they decided to leave me in Port Hueneme, California until they got ready to send me back to Chicago for discharge. I was handling gambling on the base, I was loaning money; fifty cents on the dollar and I was lending ensigns, lieutenants and the personnel the money. Now I would find out from the yeomen how the draft was going and if they were going to use from the top to the bottom and if my name was at the top the yeoman would put my name on the bottom because I was letting them have money. Now the only ones that had to pay me back were the service men that were shipping out and I knew because I got the names from the yeomen so when they got their money I was right there at the head of the class to get my money and the lieutenants and some clipper captains and the warrant officer, they didn't have to pay that extra."

The Saga of Black Navy Veterans of World War II

Hayward Howard

"My name is Hayward Howard and I'm from Lansing, Michigan and I went in the service in July 1943 and I came back to Lansing, Michigan and met this lovely lady and got married. I have been running my own business in the wall washing and window cleaning business for over forty-some years and I'm about ready to retire if I can. My service career wasn't that great. I spent a lot of time playing basketball and I ran picket boats and I was quartermaster first class when I got out. That's about it. didn't do anything great. I was in for 32 months during the war. When I was in service school the golden thirteen went to school with us two days a week right out here in Great Lakes and I met a couple of them and knew them. I knew they were in there but I didn't know what they were in there for and they didn't either which was strange. We didn't know they were going to become officers. One of them I got to know pretty well whose name was Nelson and I suppose I was the first guy who got to salute him because he looked me up. That's about the only thing that I did that was unusual. I was just an eighteen year old youngster and didn't know what I was doing."

Philip Clinton

"My name is Philip Clinton. Originally I'm from Springfield, Massachusetts and that was where I went into the service, the United States Navy. I went in in '43 right after high school graduation and I went through boot camp at Camp Lawrence. Right after finishing that I went to service school at Camp Robert Smalls. Following my term there after finishing in service school I went up to Massachusetts to the Squadam Naval Air Station. There is where I performed my engineering feats with civilians and to my credit I laid out two air fields in Massachusetts and surveyed them, working with

An American Triumph

my senior officers which one was a civilian and one was a service man. Those are the functions that I performed. In the service I learned to hang up my clothes. I learned to see the order of things. Things that were out of order was one of the things that I learned and has made me a better person to live with. One of the experiences that I had when I was aboard ship, and I had a rating but I couldn't give commands to my White counter-parts. So most of the time with the rating that I had I couldn't use it. I slept with the cooks and bakers. I couldn't sleep with the engineers that I was working with. I was in Laharue, France; we were taking the fresh troops over there and bringing the wounded back."

Anonymous Joker

"The Navy was able to teach me some discipline and it has helped quite a bit, too, and I think in terms that, when I'm talking to this now, I think in terms of when I was teaching people to interview, I used to teach interviewing, and in telling them how to respond or how to put down the answers of people generally I would say just skip over what they were saying, take down what they were saying, don't make any comment. For example, we used to have a little exercise of saying, 'What is your opinion of marijuana?' Invariably the answer would come back, 'I think it's a nice place to visit, but I wouldn't like to live there.' That's my Navy experience that's how I learned all this in the Navy. All of these things we learned in the Navy. We learned how to communicate and take surveys because then we would ask people about their qualifications and we would say, well we would want to give them easy tests so we would say, 'Name us two days in the week that begin with T.' And invariably the answer would come back, 'Today and tomorrow.' And things like that where we found many things in the Navy that helped us in our professional careers, and unfortunately, I did not see much real action because I was a specialist in athletics, I played ball most of the time although I was in the Navy, but I did like to communicate and as I say in communicating I've always remembered how you think in terms of people asking questions and the answers you get back. In addition to that marijuana thing we used to also say when Lyndon Baines Johnson was President and he was referred to as LBJ and you'd ask somebody, 'What do you think about LSD?' And they would invariably confuse the two and say, 'I voted for that s.o.b. the last time; I'll never vote for him any more.' The thing at that time we had was called a foreign policy and invariably we would ask a question like 'now I would guess our main concern would be—is it our Vietnam Policy or our Israeli policy?' And invariably the respondent would smile and he'd say, 'Oh, I really like that, but it's a little rough on my wife's elbows.'"

Milton B. Allen

"My name is Milton B. Allen from Baltimore, Maryland."

Dr. Peters: "What year did you go into the Navy?"

"October 1943."

Dr. Peters: "Now this many years later, how do you feel about your experiences in the Navy?"

"It was a unique experience I was the person who was laden with the burden of 'integrating' the personnel at Great Lakes because at that time there were three Black camps and several White camps a mile or so away across the road and when the new president came in after I went in he ordered that to be integration then; racial integration, so in answer to his direction I was sent over to the White side while a White seaman was sent to the Black side on a daily basis. So every morning they'd send a jeep over to take me over and I'd work there all day and they'd send a jeep to take me home. Same thing for the White boy. That was integration in those days. And while I was there I wrote a treatise on how racial discrimination had harmed the Navy, and nothing ever happened to it, of course, I gave it to my commanding officer. He thought it was excellent and did nothing with it. It was a very bitter experience for me just to go through this. I worked in a selection office; we had a job to assigning new recruits to various programs throughout the system. I worked there for one year. Then I was transferred to Lua Lua Lei University and Lua Lua Lei Naval Base in Hawaii, and there I established a school to teach non readers to read in 90 days and was very, very successful. My commanding officer got the money. We had six class rooms, we had a group of teachers teaching them. All educated men, and I taught them in my system and in 90 days they were reading and when the program was a success my commanding officer came in and thanked me for doing it. And he said, 'Milton, I haven't the slightest idea of what you're doing, but it's great, and I'm going to get a promotion for this.' He got some big award, I forgot what it was. He'd see me once a week and he said, 'Milton, you are doing a great job; I have no idea what you're doing because I am not an educator, but you are doing great' and he'd go on back down to the officers club. That's the way the system worked in those days. I was educated to be a teacher in Baltimore City so I knew how to teach and when I went there I saw nothing was being done so I did it. I knew I had to teach kids how to read and they learned to read in 90 days under my program and it was spread throughout the Pacific area and my commanding officer, who didn't know a darn thing that I was doing he got a huge metal. I forgot the name of it. Oh, he was excited and in various newspapers all around the country and everything and I got a metal about as big as a quarter. That's the way it was in those days. Thank God most of it's disappeared."

I lived in Baltimore, Maryland all my life and of course I lived in the segregated system so was used to it. It wasn't fair, and it wasn't honest and it wasn't realistic, but I was used to it. I was elated to at least see them make an effort to change the system. It was just a token effort, that's all it was. I don't know whether they eventually changed it or not because I finally went to Hawaii to teach school and teach kids how to read, and I don't know what happened at Great Lakes after that, but it's one of the cruelties of our system. The waste of manpower, waste of brain power. Segregation hurts a lot. Still hurts. But nobody's willing to face it. They're not willing to face the fact that you've wasted manpower and brain power. It's a horrible fact in our society. Doing us a lot of damage. I mean us as a nation, not us as a race."

Interviewer: "When did you go to law school?"

"As soon as I came out of the service, 1945."

Interviewer: "Where was that?"

"University of Maryland School of Law, I was the fourth Black admitted to that school. I was the fourth Black, Murray, Douglas, Perkins and Allen — we helped integrate the school and of course I finished school in two and a half years and took the bar exam and became a lawyer even before I finished school. Although I was a bona fide lawyer I had to go back and take another half year of college to get my qualifications, then I became a lawyer, then I became a prosecutor, chief prosecutor for Baltimore, then I became a judge. Served as a judge for ten years and I've retired recently. My life in the Navy was a very bitter experience but I'm used to that as a Black man. I think things have changed dramatically since then." When I went to Hawaii I was assigned to teach the illiterates how to read and we had a camp place called Lua Lua Lei, Hawaii and it was an ammunition dump and there was a lot of illiterates there so when they learned what my qualifications were they asked me would I teach them how to read."

Lewis Williams

My name is Lewis Williams. I'm from Chicago. I went into the Navy on July tenth, 1942. I got to Great Lakes. Fortunately one of the men who I had gone to school with at the University of Chicago was head of personnel and so when he saw me he said, "What do you plan to do in the Navy, there's nothing in the Navy for you." So I said, "You're here, so there must be something for me." So after my boot training when I had my leave I visited him in his office and we decided that the ability he would make for me was head of the classification office and so from that point on I headed classification, and that was before they integrated the Navy. Jim Peters will tell you that I had an illiterate program. Many of the Blacks that came into the Navy in that period were from the south and they didn't read or write, and so what had happened, one night I had the duty, I was responsible for anything that happened on the base during my particular period. I got a call that there were some Blacks over at the main gate and they had to be picked up. It was bitterly cold. I couldn't arouse the truck driver and I knew those guys were not properly clothed so I got the truck and I had never driven a truck, but I managed to go over to the main side and pick up these recruits and bring them back to Camp Smalls and then when also it was my responsibility to assign them pay numbers and to have them sign the check. Most of them couldn't sign their names. The next morning I asked Commander Armstrong if he would permit me, I would like to have a school, so these poor guys that can't read and write will be able to be something to themselves and to the Navy. Because most of these guys were sent them to the Army if they couldn't read and write. He gave me permission. I said extend their service period here at the Great Lakes from eight to twelve weeks and I feel I can teach them how to read and write in twelve weeks. He said, 'You think you can do it? Okay.' So I did and the school was successful and we had a lot of fun. I think we graduated thousands."

Dr. Peters: "Mr. Williams got me into the remedial education program, he and the late William Thomas were the persons who pulled me into the program under the chaplaincy and they left the program with me. He and Bill Thomas were the key people who helped to organize the Blacks in the Navy at Camp Robert Smalls. They set the tone."

James T. Howard

"I live on Hyannis, Cape Cod, Massachusetts. I went into the Navy at Great Lakes, I was the 126th man to get there under that program where we trained 60 to 70 thousand Black sailors. I was in the second company. There was form there. I arrived there on June the twelfth, 1942. Remember that! And from there I went to the service school. Quartermaster signalman. And after that I got a quartermaster third class rating and I stayed in ships company Great Lakes until November 1943 when I was sent to Corpus Christi and one of the unique experiences I had down there they would send me and about four or five White boys out on this mine sweep up for training every day and at lunch time I would sit down with them at the table and eat lunch, but at night time when I came back I had to eat dinner by myself because I was the only Black on the base. So from there I went with the mine sweep up to Galveston, Texas and I finished up my Navy career there."

Interviewer: "How did they know you were Black because you're very light skinned."

"My hair, there was no question about that I never was able to fool anybody on that question."

My home town was Philadelphia at that time. I was very happy because I was 1A as the draft board and the Army was breathing down my neck. I did not want to go into the Army I wanted to go into the Navy so I was actually really sweating it out until June first came along. I was down to that recruiting station at 8:00 in the morning when it opened up. So I was very happy about that when it came. Of course, I took the physical and they said well you go home, we will call you and I didn't hear from them for a number of days when my greetings from the President of the United States came to report for the Army and I ran down to the recruiting station and they said 'well, oh gee, the only thing that we don't have back is your blood test.' They called the naval hospital and they said it was all right. Now this was a Friday around 10:00, they said you'll go away tonight, 6:00. I said, 'Oh now wait a minute how about swearing me in and letting me wait a week.' They said, 'no.'"

Interviewer: "You're one of the founders of this organization."

"Yes, I'm co-founder with Jim Peters."

Interviewer: "How did you feel when you knew that ball was going to be cast, you said that you were ready on June first, how did you feel?"

"Well, I read about it in the papers that Roosevelt, and this was in April when he signed his executive order that Negroes were going to be able to go into the general service, so I was just really sweating it out until June first. So when that recruiting station opened up I was right down there. I always figured that if I was in the Army and the bomb hit the field kitchen, I would be no more good as a fighting man because I was hungry. And I knew I was going to eat if I was in the Navy."

Chapter 4

Organizing Black World War II Navy Veterans of Great Lakes The Beginning — September 1982

During the winter of 1981-1982 Dr. James S. Peters, II, his late wife Marie, my wife, Agatha, and I were sitting at the kitchen table at our home on Cape Cod, Massachusetts and it was mentioned that although members of other branches of the armed services held reunions the former sailors of Great Lakes had never held one.

Thus began the planning for the first reunion of the World War II Black Navy Veterans of Great Lakes. It was held at the Ambassador East Hotel in Chicago September 24 and 25, 1982.

Included with this packet of materials of our early beginnings are the program of that reunion and the list of the 44 members who comprised the first group. Also is a form which was sent out to all of the former Navy men that we knew of to contact other former sailors.*

James T. Howard
Cofounder and Permanent Board Member
Dr. James S. Peters, II
Cofounder

* See Appendix 3

The Saga of Black Navy Veterans of World War II

In the fall of 1977 I accepted a Distinguished Visiting Professorship in Rehabilitation at Southern Illinois University, Carbondale to assist in establishing the nation's first doctoral program of rehabilitation. This appointment was for the school year. My late wife, Marie, also received an appointment as Associate Professor of Human Development in the Child and Family Studies Department.

While at S.I.U., Carbondale I met some former Navy shipmates who had been members of the Great Lakes Navy Band. Notably, Drs. Samuel A. Floyd, Jr., Clifford D. Harper and Malvin E. Moore. I had heard about them from my friends Dr. Huel Perkins and Walter Mines of my alma mater, Southern University in Louisiana. Both had played in the band at Great Lakes and had told me of a special reunion by former band members at S.I.U., Carbondale. According to Floyd:[1]

> In the spring of 1973, forty-eight men, all former musicians, met at Southern Illinois university at Carbondale, Illinois for a reunion. These men, some with their wives and children, came from as far away as Seattle, Washington; Itta Bena, Mississippi, and New York City. They are a few of the hundreds of Black Navy musicians who were stationed at the Great Lakes Naval Training Center at some time during the years 1942-1945. These men were coming together as a group for the first time since World War II.

While conducting a workshop at my alma mater, Southern University, Baton Rouge, Louisiana in 1979 my friend Dr. Huel D. Perkins, then Dean, School of Humanities, a former member of the Great Lakes Band, told me more of the reunion of former members the past year. He said that my friend Walter Mines, a member of the business department at Southern, who also had been a member of the band at Great Lakes had tape recorded the sessions. After hearing the tapes and talking to them about how successful the reunion had been I decided that with help, I could organize a reunion of World War II Black Navy Veterans of Great Lakes to celebrate the fortieth (40th) anniversary (1982) of our enlistment. We would have a couple of years to get ready for it.

Upon returning home to Storrs, Connecticut I contacted a good friend and former shipmate, James Howard, who had moved from Boston, Massachusetts to Hyannis, to discuss the idea of a fortieth (40th) reunion of our shipmates with him. The reunion would be to commemorate 1942, the year of the acceptance of Blacks into general service of the Navy.

Jim and I worked for over two years on this project. Our wives gave their full support. We enlisted help from President Reagan; the Department of Defense; The Navy Department and the Command at Great Lakes Naval Training Center. Many former shipmates all over the country, north, south, east and west were contacted and responded positively. The celebration was held in Chicago and at Great Lakes in 1982. We were quartered in the famous Ambassador East Hotel of Chicago, and through a friend and financier, formerly of Hartford, Roy Jackson, had special use of the Famous Pump Room. Mr. Jackson rented a suite for Marie and me to entertain our Chicago friends and my shipmates, their wives and children.

The highlight of the reunion was our welcome back to Great Lakes where we were guests of the Commander and his staff. The regimental review and graduation was dedicated to us. I was guest speaker at a special luncheon at the Officer's Club. We were wined and dined throughout the day. Our banquet was excellent. It was difficult to believe that after forty years we were so honored. A dream had been realized.

At our business meeting the next day in Chicago we voted to form an organization. The name voted on and accepted was: World War II Black Navy Veterans of Great Lakes. We made plans to meet once each year and to open our membership to all Navy veterans of Great Lakes. Officers elected were:

> James Howard, President
> James S. Peters, II, Secretary
> Vulcan Taylor, Treasurer

Plans were made to have chapters over the country. Two chapters came into being at that meeting. They were Chicago and Detroit. The Chicago chapter was designated the mother chapter and Chicago the major seat of our reunion. Other cities could request a reunion of the group and be considered.

Now after nine reunions we decided to have a gala tenth to celebrate the fiftieth (50th) anniversary of our entrance into the Navy's general service at Great Lakes and Camp Robert Smalls.

On June 18 to 20, 1992 Black Navy Veterans of World War II gathered at the Hyatt Regency Hotel in Chicago to commemorate and celebrate that historic event. We were, as per usual, invited to Great Lakes Naval Training Center for part of the celebration. We were pleased to see so many Black officers and recruits. We were happy to learn that a Black Navy officer would shortly become the Commander of the center. We experienced the usual hospitality on the base as honored guests.

On the evening of the banquet Professor Janet Macy of the University of Minnesota, who was my invited guest, taped the proceedings, and tape interviewed a number of those present.

Organizing Black Navy Veterans of WWII at Great Lakes

We wanted to explore the impact their experience had on them and their families and to create a record of this historically important time.

This book is a summation of the experiences of some of the American Black Navy Veterans who served their country faithfully and well in spite of the adversity of segregation and discrimination.

Appendix 1

The Special Training Program

The educational standard for induction into the Armed Forces has changed from time to time, but it has generally meant the ability to read and write English at about the fourth grade level. A man must have a reasonable amount of education to be of value to the services. Waging modern war is a much more complex undertaking than the fighting of past years. The modern Army and Navy are highly mechanized with such equipment as planes, tanks, radio, rockets, and the almost fabulously intricate war machine which is the present day battleship, cruiser or submarine. The man who cannot read and follow simple written directions is hampered in the proper handling of such equipment. He is also a hazard to himself and to those with whom he might be associated.

—"Leadership & The Negro Soldier,"
M5 Army Service Force Manual, 1944

Selective Service drew men from all walks of life, and all selectees were subjected to neuropsychiatric examinations at the induction centers before being accepted for military service. Since the standards as formulated were the same for every individual irrespective of race, it might be assumed that the Negro-White populations in the military services would break down into two comparable racial population groups, representative except for the fact that the neuropsychiatrically unfit and the mentally unfit had been removed from each group.

However, similar selection standards for intelligence were not uniformly applied to both groups in the Navy. The standards for the selection of Negroes were often more lenient than those for White recruits. Thus in the induction of Negro illiterates — as in the case of Negro service school men under patterns of segregation — comparison of military performance with a corresponding White group was biased and weighted. Throwing a more carefully selected group into social competition with a less carefully selected one proved detrimental to improved race relations. It could hardly favor the development of mutual tolerance and understanding.

In June 1943, the U.S. Navy reluctantly agreed to admit its fair share of illiterates under Selective Service. Although this was the first recognition of the fact that the naval service would have to make room for enlisted personnel who could not read and write, a great number of men of this category had already come into the service on a voluntary basis and were scattered throughout the naval establishment. Immediately after Pearl Harbor, recruiting stations were released from the obligation of administrating the General Classification Test to applicants — and since this regulation remained in abeyance until the beginning of 1945, a very large number of illiterates found their way into the Navy through normal recruiting channels. As early as February 28, 1942, a recruiting circular letter called attention to the fact that large numbers of illiterates were being received at recruit training centers, and directed that recruiting officers should administer an intelli-

Appendix 1. The Special Training Program

gence test when there was any doubt of an applicant's educational qualifications.

The presence of a growing body of illiterates in the naval establishment created a training problem which the Navy was wholly unprepared to deal with. Prior to the war, this problem was non-existent; and there is a good deal of evidence to show that the authorities were most reluctant to accept the responsibility for setting up any special literacy training programs for a long time after the need for such programs had become obvious. Yet, the highly specialized nature of nearly every type of naval duty made it virtually obligatory that the humblest seaman should have some reading knowledge. Writing of this problem in August 1945 to the U.S. Commissioner of Education, The Director of Training set forth in detail the advantages and problems of the Navy's Special Training Program:

1. At times the period allowed for recruit training was contracted by the demands of the service to four or five weeks. Under these circumstances the trainee was obliged to acquire a large part of his instruction through reading. It was found that it took approximately four times as long to train an illiterate to perform an average Navy job as it did one who could read.

2. The establishment of a training program which did not depend on the use of printed matter would have been both difficult and expensive. Experience showed that it was simpler and more economical to teach men to read than to devise materials which did not require this knowledge.

3. The establishment of a smooth administrative routine was greatly complicated by the presence of non-readers. A system for the rapid handling of records was a virtual impossibility where men could not fill out information blanks, pay receipts, beneficiary forms, allotment cards, et cetera.

4. Sufficient education to read safety precautions was essential for men working with machinery, high explosives, and heavy cargo. Serious accidents were traced directly to the inability of men to read warnings and study safety instructions.

5. A social barrier of serious implication was found to exist between literate and illiterate personnel.

6. The administrative dualism resulting from putting literates and illiterates together caused much confusion. Literates tended to resent the long oral directions which they had to listen to for the sake of the illiterates in their number.

7. A large number of minor disciplinary problems were the direct outgrowth of misunderstandings caused by the inability to read station orders, watch bills, leave and liberty regulations, and safety precautions.

8. The inability to read and write letters constituted a serious morale problem among illiterates, and the consequent obstacle to satisfactory adjustment to naval life. It became increasingly evident that a knowledge of reading and writing helped overcome feelings of inferiority, and tended to develop initiative, aggressiveness, and more willing acceptance of the conditions of military life.

The Navy was extremely slow, however, in recognizing that illiteracy constituted a serious personnel problem, involving dislocations of the kind listed above. It was not until July 2, 1943, that the Bureau of Naval Personnel took any official cognizance of the situation. On that date a letter was dispatched to the training stations authorizing the retention of men who could not read and write English on special details beyond the usual time in order to permit them to acquire a working knowledge of the language. It should be noted that in this directive the Bureau refrained from establishing a regular literacy program, or even from indicating what means should

Appendix 1. The Special Training Program

be taken to provide this essential working knowledge. At this time such literacy training as was carried on at the recruit training stations was conducted on an extra-curricular basis, after hours, by volunteer instructors. These instructors were inexperienced in most cases, had at their disposal no adequate teaching materials and were themselves recruits in training.

By late summer of 1943, the assignment of illiterates to general service had begun to create situations which the Bureau of Naval Personnel could no longer ignore. On September 30, NTS, Norfolk, reported to the Bureau that illiterates were being received from boot camps in increasing numbers. Since all the facilities of this station at that time were needed for destroyer and destroyer escort training, permission was requested to transfer illiterates to Bainbridge, Maryland, for further literacy instruction and subsequent assignment to the steward's branch. Apparently the Bureau granted this permission without giving due consideration to the practical consequences of such a decision. The result was that Bainbridge found itself deluged with illiterates which it had no facilities for handling. On November 26, 1943, Bainbridge informed the Bureau that it had on hand 156 Negro illiterates received from other stations, and that this number was increasing at an average rate of thirty each week. The Bureau was requested to clarify its policy toward illiterates, or at the very least, to send representatives to review the situation. By this time, the Training Division of the Bureau had begun to turn its attention to the establishment of a special training program, but the only immediate result of the appeal from Bainbridge was a cancellation by the Bureau of the permission to transfer illiterates from Norfolk to Bainbridge. The Bureau stated that because of the acute shortage of men, the illiterates would have to be absorbed in the destroyer and destroyer escort training programs.

By the end of 1943, the Bureau could no longer close its eyes to a situation which it had only complicated and confused by makeshift solutions. With Planning and Control applying the spur, the Training Division rushed into print a series of instructional pamphlets together with a twelve-week curriculum for illiterates. An airmailgram of December 22, 1943, announced the imminent appearance of a special course in recruit training, but directed that all commands continue to accept illiterates for general service prior to the establishment of this course. On the following day Great Lakes was instructed to be ready to receive by January 3, 1944, an initial draft of 420 White illiterates as advanced guard of an influx which was expected to swell to 5,000.

At the same time it was announced that a similar program for Negro illiterates would be set up as soon as adequate space and instructors could be made available. Once in operation, the school for Whites was transferred from Great Lakes to Camp Peary, Williamsburg, Virginia. This was in March 1944. At this time plans called for a weekly input of up to 500 trainees with a total capacity of 6,000. But a month later, the total enrollment in the Camp Peary school was 10,000.

The establishment of special training at Camp Peary for Whites, and at Great Lakes for Negroes in the early months of 1944, provided for the handling of illiterates on a recruit level, but did nothing for the thousands of illiterates who had already passed through basic training. The task of teaching these men to read and write was delegated to the commanding officers of training stations, ships and forward area bases, who were allowed full liberty to handle the matter in whatever way they deemed best. The refusal of the Bureau of Naval Personnel to undertake any responsibility for qualifying the thousands of illiterates who had been admitted to the Navy prior to 1944

Appendix 1. The Special Training Program

was explicitly stated in the Circular Letter 176-44 of February 4, 1944, which stated in part:

> Illiterates now in training or in general service... will not be transferred to the Special Training Units. Extra-curricular programs already in operation will continue to function as long as there is need. Materials for this purpose will be furnished by this Bureau upon official request.

In offering to supply training materials suitable for instructing illiterates, however, the Bureau was promising what it could not deliver throughout the greater part of 1944; and without any centralized administrative control over the recommended extracurricular courses, the disposition of illiterates above the recruit level continued to be a sore spot in the entire program. Yet, in a second circular letter dated July 2, 1944, The Bureau reaffirmed its unwillingness to tackle the question of what was to be done with a large backlog of illiterates built up through 1943. There followed to all naval activities an express prohibition of the transfer of illiterates to Camp Peary, which was to be maintained only as a recruit training station. Suitable billets had to be assigned such illiterates at their present stations; and again, it was directed that activities should whenever possible carry on their own remedial training on an extracurricular basis, with the Bureau supplying curricula and training materials on request. The Bureau continued until 1945 to refrain from assuming administrative control over the training of illiterates above the recruit level.

Originally, the Navy sent most of the illiterates into the steward's branch. As the quotas of stewards reached the saturation point, subsequent large numbers of illiterates had to be absorbed by other training activities. The adjustment of these men in general training was even more difficult than that in the steward's branch. In 1943 and 1944 the Negro illiterates at Great Lakes comprised one percent of the incoming Negro recruits; by late 1945, the number of Negro illiterates soared to 31 percent.

The problems of the Negro illiterate recruits were first handled by the chaplain's office and the education officer in each of the Negro camps at Great Lakes. This was done with fair success as an "after hours" project during the late months of 1943 and the early months of 1944—and while the number of Negro illiterates was comparatively small. But as the Navy was forced to accept more and more Negro illiterates via Selective Service, the number of men needing remedial training rapidly outgrew the facilities. By April 1944, formal school organization had been set up, and a remedial school with adequate space and volunteer recruit teachers (under the supervision of a nucleus of ship's company staff members of the school) had been procured. In both Camp Lawrence and Camp Moffett, a small administration building and a complete barracks converted entirely for classroom activities was set aside for remedial school work.

Text books, teaching materials, training aids, teaching methods, testing, curriculum—all had to be devised in lieu of any standardized materials from the Bureau. The three R's were taught on a grade-school level but couched completely within the recruit training program. Much of the material to be covered during the period of recruit training was conducted within the school to facilitate the training of these handicapped men. Emphasis was placed throughout the curriculum upon the history and background of the U.S. Navy, the Negro's part in the service, and the importance of each man in

Appendix 1. The Special Training Program

the development and maintenance of the world's foremost fighting machine, the U.S. Navy.

As the service schools for Negroes in Camp Smalls came to an end, the Special Training Unit gradually took over their facilities, and by November 1944 the whole school was housed in the spacious service school buildings. The school enrollment at that time numbered 1,800 men.

In the remedial school days, the illiterates were members of all the companies in the Negro regiments, and were drawn out of their companies for remedial work in keeping with the individual company's recruit training schedule. The teachers were drawn from the same companies, most of whom volunteered for such duty during their boot training period.

In the formation of the special training school, the illiterates comprised a complete battalion and operated independently of any other recruit training unit. They attended classes on a regular schedule set up for each company. All teachers were members of ship's company and functioned with greater efficiency with their wider range of experience, training and indoctrination in the Navy Special Training Unit curriculum.

Greater care was taken in the selection of battalion and company officers, company commanders and petty officers. In fact the units had better leadership in the company officers, and better prepared and conscientious recruit petty officers than any recruit company in the Negro regiments. Every phase of recruit training that could be taught within the school was done, and the illiterates were instructed at their levels the techniques they were to be taught under the auspices of other agencies in the recruit training command.

Originally recruit training was of eight weeks duration— and regardless of the student's status in the remedial school he was shipped out according to schedule and he graduated with the rest of his company. In the Special Training Unit, remedial students were kept for a period of 12 weeks—to cover Navy recruit indoctrination and to acquire minimum standards of literacy.

Recruits in the Special Training Unit who were retarded and who failed to make the grade during the twelve-week period, were kept for a total of sixteen weeks; those who failed to make fifth grade level after the second period could be retained up to twenty weeks, if, in the opinion of the school administration, the man or men were of sufficient caliber to retain them. Of fifteen thousand men passing through the school less than twenty-five had to be retained for the full period of sixteen weeks and none were kept longer.

Upon arrival at Great Lakes, all Negro recruits except the college men and high-school graduates were subjected to a literacy test. Those who passed were sent directly to normal recruit training companies. Those who failed but could probably read and write a little were given the Kent Oral Examination. Those who passed were sent into the Special Training Unit for remedial training. Those who failed were sent to the medical department and the staff psychiatrist and psychologist who administered other neuropsychiatric and psychometric testing. Those who passed the tests and proved to be above mental deficiency levels were sent over to the Special Training Unit for "Trial Duty." Those who failed to make sufficient progress by the end of the twelve-week period were discharged and released. The staff of psychiatrists also passed final judgement on the "trial duty" failures before they were dismissed from the service. Petty Officer James Peters was a member of the psychology group and represented the Special Training Unit.

Appendix 1. The Special Training Program

The majority of Negro illiterates were inducted from twelve Southern states, and these had the most limited educational systems in America:

Alabama	Kentucky	South Carolina
Arkansas	Louisiana	Tennessee
Florida	Mississippi	Texas
Georgia	North Carolina	Virginia

These twelve states furnished 66 percent of all the men tested, and 91 percent of those requiring remedial training and sent to the Special Training Unit.

Composition of the school was developed on the basis of four levels of teaching: Remedials, Near-Illiterates, Illiterates and Non-Readers; and the four levels were determined in grades made in the literacy or placement tests. For a six-month period, cumulative records showed that the proportion of men in each learning bracket was about the same as monthly figures, although the school population had continued to increase monthly over the same period.

The direct application of the things learned in school aroused considerable interest on the part of the recruit students, and created the desire to cooperate and to learn. Newspaper publicity, pictures and announcements of their achievements, and the encouragement given through camp periodicals in addition to personal awards received aided immeasurable as incentives to learn.

In addition to the three R;s, recruit illiterates began to understand the fundamentals of citizenship, such as the value and significance of the franchise, and many actually registered and voted as absentees from their voting districts for the first time. Many men related the experiences and problems of their recent tenant farm days, and expressed gratitude for the opportunities afforded them through the Navy to learn to read and write, which would in turn aid in computing crop returns, and the money owed and due that had heretofore been left entirely to the honesty and presumed integrity of their White landowners and employers.

Questioned about their lack of education and why they hadn't attended school during adolescence or for longer periods, it was found that the vast majority had resided in small rural communities and often far removed from schools; others were the oldest or sole male support of large families; others just failed to see any advantage in going to school. Some had taken jobs at early ages; others had been "farmed out" by their families in an effort to survive a meager existence. In any large group of southern rural Negroes one expects to find complacency and a general state of illiteracy among the older men, but surprisingly enough the younger men provided the most acute problems of illiteracy due to sheer ignorance and indifference.

Morale was exceptionally high in the Special Training Unit; and gradually the illiterates began to excel not only within the confines of the school and their company units, but also in general competition with other recruit companies. Previously, in the old remedial school set-up, these illiterates had borne the brunt of ridicule. They were called "knuckle-heads" because of the difficulties they had encountered in recruit training with normal recruits, and they usually held no responsible positions in their companies, and as often as not fell heir to the dirtiest and most distasteful jobs of their respective units. Under the Special Training Program these same men soon became the best disciplined, the most cooperative, and the finest drilled companies among Negro recruit units at Great Lakes; had the outstanding

Appendix 1. The Special Training Program

amateur athletes, and were the frequent recipients of the major incentive, competitive and achievement awards presented to the Negro units. With opportunity to learn and compete, assume responsibility and a chance to earn respect with new avenues for expression and recognition, these men made phenomenal progress and exceptional achievements in school.

The presence of Negro officers in key positions throughout the Negro camps helped immeasurably to inspire the illiterates as well as the other Negro recruits at the base. In fact, these officers did all possible to encourage and assist the illiterates to find themselves in their respective fields of work. The students of the Special Training Unit were exceptionally proud of their school and company officers, their battery of Negro instructors, Negro company commanders and petty officers, and the Negro officers they came in daily contact with in Personnel, Classification, Athletics, Public Relations and the Chaplain's Office. (Ensign Reginald Goodwin, Personnel & Classification, Great Lakes; Ensign Samuel Barnes, Athletic Department; Ensign Phillip Barnes, Out-Going Unit; Lt(jg) James Brown, Chaplain; Lt(jg) Thomas Parham, Chaplain; Bo'sn. Louis Johnson, Company Commander; Lt (jg) Arthur Thompson, (MC); Ensign Dennis D. Nelson, OinC, Special Training Unit.)

Late in 1945, and in keeping with policies and directives of the Navy Department, integration of all units began to take place. The Special Training Program continued to be carried on at Camp Peary and at Great Lakes, until orders arrived which consolidated the two units at Camp Peary. Additional training at Bainbridge and Red Bank, New Jersey, for Negro illiterates in the steward's branch was provided in evening classes. As the "Navy Life" texts and workbooks, arithmetic and the revised curriculum appeared, they were gradually incorporated into the courses of study at each of the special training schools.

Meanwhile, the backlog of illiterates and semi-illiterates constituted an increasingly critical problem at numerous activities where there were no facilities for offering additional training of the type called for. Reports indicated that the majority of illiterates made available for general service duty were assigned to air stations, ammunition and supply depots and naval magazines. Unfortunately, the men at these stations were constantly called upon to work with highly dangerous explosives, inflammables and machinery, so that their duties were precisely the type that necessitated reading knowledge if essential safety precautions were to be effective. Since activities of the sort listed above did not come under Bureau of Naval Personnel jurisdiction, such remedial training as was undertaken had to be conducted on a voluntary "after hours" basis.

Outside the large naval training centers and bases with their formal programs of literacy training, Negro and White illiterates were frequently found in considerable numbers in units offering very limited educational opportunities. Many such units attempted to incorporate some type of literacy training for their illiterate personnel. From large and small outfits conducting such programs, some interesting facts and correlations were obtained. It was found that Negroes and Whites made similar scores on various measures of progress in learning the three R's; that the learning of Negroes and Whites from the North, where educational opportunities had been relatively better for both groups, was more rapid and effective than for those from the South. One thing they both had in common: whether Negro or White, whether from the North or South—they all had been victims of very meager educational opportunities and low cultural status. Data con-

Appendix 1. The Special Training Program

firmed the idea that low cultural status lessened the expression of ability to such an extent that the results of mental tests devised by the Navy were wholly inadequate as indicators of "intelligence" or "learning ability." The conspicuous and rapid learning of Negroes and Whites under the Special Training Program in the Navy far exceeded the expectations for either group.

Data from the Army's Special Training Program confirmed the Navy's belief for the hypothesis that "Negroes and Whites of comparable backgrounds (i.e., subcultural environment, including poor schools) appeared to learn with approximately equal effectiveness." (*The Journal of Abnormal & Social Psychology,* October 1946, Paul Whitty.) Hence, it was. proven "in the field" that Negroes and Whites of similar backgrounds do, when given similar educational opportunity and motive, make similar progress and learn with equal ease. The Army and the Navy were taught the heartening lesson that if learning ability is taken as a criterion of intelligence, great groups of underprivileged American citizens (Negro, White and non-English speaking) often thought of as uneducable, are "intelligent," i.e., capable of learning far beyond the expectations set by "intelligence" tests. In fact, the unusual learning ability demonstrated by Negroes and Whites under special training was entirely in accord with the conclusions of many educators and investigators who believe that intelligence tests provide a very inadequate and unreliable measure of real ability of individuals in low cultural groups. At any rate, they definitely concluded that the results of such tests should never be employed for comparison of the "intelligence" of racial groups.

By the autumn of 1944, the Instructor Training Section of the Bureau of Naval Personnel was fully organized and operating smoothly. The Special Training Program offered a fertile field into which to extend its administrative functions, and an opening was providentially provided when the Naval Air Station at Corpus Christi invited the Bureau to set up a training program for a large number of Negro and White illiterates on duty at that station. An officer from the Instructor Training Section was detailed to Corpus Christi, and during a three-month period, he established a special training program with the enthusiastic cooperation of the station authorities. He was also able to try out and prove the Navy Life, Book I (the basic text material of the course) as a satisfactory workbook for the instruction of illiterates. The course put into effect at Corpus Christi served as a model for the subsequent projects of the Instructor Training Section in this sphere of Navy training.

By January 1945, the basic teaching materials for the special training program were ready; and in February 1945 the Bureau finally called on all commandants of naval districts to conduct a survey to determine the number of personnel assigned to duties within their commands whose knowledge of reading was below the level of fourth grade. This directive neglected to specify either what constituted the required literacy standard or how the men who fell below it were to be singled out; and, as a result, the reports received were wholly inconclusive. Even so, estimates received from 130 activities listed 3,391 illiterates. This figure would surely have been much higher if proper testing methods had been used for the determination of personnel whose reading knowledge was fourth grade level or lower. No accurate records were ever kept that would make it possible to make even approximate guesses as to the number of illiterates who were admitted to the Navy during World War II. In November 1944 it was estimated, however, that about 6 percent of all recruits fell below the fifth-grade level in literacy, (This figure compares

Appendix 1. The Special Training Program

favorably with the percentage of illiteracy in the nation's population as revealed by the 1940 Census. At that time 3.8 percent of the population 35 years of age and over had no schooling, and 9.9 percent had 1-4 years of grade school education.) of which percentage half could be classified as trainable in reading. In the nine-month period between November 1944 and August 1945, 55,000 to 60,000 copies of the literacy program textbook, Navy Life, Book I, were distributed for use in connection with literacy training.

The reports from the naval districts did not give a satisfactory indication of the scope on which special training should be undertaken, but they did clearly show that there was an urgent need for such a program. Accordingly, a representative of the Instructor Training Section was sent into the field to develop the possibilities of training for illiterates. This officer progressed from district to district, visiting naval activities where the presence of illiterates was creating critical problems, and explained the facilities which the Bureau of Naval Personnel was prepared to make available for remedial work. In reality, his prime mission was to "sell" the Special Training Program, since, as has been pointed out, the majority of illiterates were detailed to air stations, ammunition depots and similar activities over which the Bureau of Naval Personnel had no direct control. In addition, testing procedures for the location of men who did not meet the required literacy standards instituted in accordance with a system developed by the Bureau, were still in the planning stage.

The response to this initial appeal was highly gratifying, and the Instructor Training Section set about building an administrative organization adequate to the demands of the Special Training Program. A staff of two officers and eleven specialists, four of them chiefs and the remainder first class petty officers, was exclusively charged with controlling the program from the Bureau end. The two officers acted in a general supervisory capacity, while the specialists went into each naval district and made actual arrangements for setting up special training courses in the activities which had signified their willingness to conduct such training. These specialists were indoctrinated in their duties by a special two-week course at the Camp Peary School, followed by an additional four-week period at the Bureau in gaining familiarity with the Navy Life textbook series. Thereafter, these men went immediately into the field and assumed responsibility for setting up special training programs under the district instructor training officers. In the initial stage it was necessary to arrange for classroom space and all related facilities, and to select and train instructors. There followed a period of assisting in the development of the course and supervising its performance before each Specialist proceeded to repeat this performance at another activity.

Perhaps the principal problem attendant on the efficient functioning of special training for illiterates was the choice of teachers who had suitable temperamental and educational qualifications for the type of teaching required, and who were willing to volunteer for the duty. At the outset, the Bureau specialists, themselves, undertook to indoctrinate candidates in the proper techniques of the Navy Life books. Later, however, teachers chosen for the special training program were ordered to Great Lakes, where they had an opportunity to observe an established school in operation (Camp Robert Smalls), and where they were able to participate in the instruction under expert supervision.

A further duty of the Bureau representatives was to place in effect a working curriculum at each activity offering training for illiterates. The problem differed with each activity. Taking account of local conditions, the specialists worked out individual schedules in terms of the Navy Life text and

Appendix 1. The Special Training Program

workbooks, likewise using the standard Bureau curriculum for special training as a model on which to determine time allowances. As a general rule, it was recommended that not less than one hundred and twenty hours be allocated for instruction in reading and writing, and that at least two hours daily be devoted to these subjects, in order that a complete course be run in a three-month's period. Unfortunately, many stations were either unwilling or unable to set aside more than an hour in a day's schedule for this teaching, although this meant the retention of illiterates at a station for six months, an unduly long period to keep a class together within ship's company complement at any command.

The Special Training Program rapidly expanded, extending throughout the naval establishment within the continental limits of the United States; the first really broadly-based system for the teaching of illiterates to be set up. The response to the Bureau's Special Training Program was extremely varied, ranging from enthusiasm to apathy. The situation was directly traceable to the fact that the Bureau lacked the authority to put the training of illiterates on a compulsory basis. As long as it was left to each separate command to decide whether it would promote this training vigorously, lend half-hearted support, or decline to participate at all, any program to enforce literacy standards throughout the naval establishment was inevitably destined to partial failure. Certain stations, however, were attended by serious difficulties. At some stations the daily work-load was so heavy that instruction had to be conducted, if at all, after hours, when the men were weary and not inclined or receptive to one or two hours of classroom activities. Likewise, the turnover of enlisted personnel at other activities, such as receiving stations, was so rapid that it was next to impossible to conduct courses of any duration without overburdening the ship's company.

Another obstacle was the Bureau's decree that illiteracy did not constitute sufficient grounds for transferring a man from one station to another. This meant that in activities where no provisions had been made for teaching reading and writing, the illiterate was deprived of all effective opportunity to learn these skills elsewhere.

The only solution to the problem would have been for the Navy to perfect its screening procedures to the point where no recruit would have been allowed to leave boot camp until he had fully met the literacy standards of the service.

The Special Training Program for Negro recruits under the auspices of the Great Lakes Naval Training Station met with unprecedented and unmatched success. Probably the chief reason for this success was due to the nature and background of the students themselves. Many of the fifteen thousand men trained in this school had no previous chance for formal education. For many, camp and school life offered a decided improvement to their former environments. Their regular eating and sleeping habits, improvement in general health and standard of living, opportunity to learn and achieve—all these gave the impetus necessary for their interest and progress. Thus the Special Training Unit provided for these men opportunities which had hitherto been denied them. Most of the men were deeply appreciative of these privileges, and recognized the responsibilities that went with their acceptance.

The Navy proved to its satisfaction the desirable effects obtained in a program of this sort. For the first time in the Navy, adults who were found to be functionally illiterate were given the opportunity to learn to read and write. The results obtained in its Special Training Units did much to refute the theory of innate Negro inferiority. From studies and facts, the Navy has concluded ("United States Naval Administration in World War II," *BuPers*.):

Appendix 1. The Special Training Program

1. That the educational achievement of Negroes above the average, indicate that the attainments of these individuals as measured by standard tests, school records, and rank in graduation are similar to those of Whites of comparable intelligence.
2. That in the field of racial differences, "race superiority" and "inferiority" have not been demonstrated despite the existence of clearly defined and tested differences between individuals within every race.
3. That the differences revealed by intelligence tests and other devices can be accounted for in terms of differences in opportunity and background. The important consideration at this point that the Navy made, was how to offer increased opportunities—both physical and cultural—to all handicapped groups, regardless of race, since these variables account in large part for poor performance and achievement in every group. The solution to this problem lay in giving each man his chance to show what he could do.
4. That scientific evidence does not support the theory that racial inferiorities exist as inborn traits, but there are differences in customs, experience, education and behavior between racial groups, as there are differences between individuals within any group.

Nelson reviewed the problems that Negro personnel faced during World War II.

During World War II, as in previous wars, the Navy experienced but few instances of serious disciplinary problems among its Negro personnel. Historically, the Navy never had cause to question the loyalty of Negroes nor was there any organized collective resistance against conditions and treatment in naval service. The few major disturbances experienced during World War II grew out of what the participants regarded as intolerable social conditions and unfair treatment—conditions which they sought to remedy or to openly resist in one form or another. Most of these disturbances might be better described as "breaches of tranquillity," but a few were of such proportions as to be considered as mutinies or riots under Navy interpretation.

Most of the disciplinary cases among Negro personnel were based on charges of disobedience or insubordination, which, although the accused probably were not aware of it, were classed among the more serious offenses of Navy Regulations. None of the mutinies were accompanied by violence typical of those occasionally experienced by the U.S. Army.

The Navy's early policy of segregation and "special treatment" and the narrow interpretations of directives and regulations by commanding officers and their subordinates were largely responsible for most of these difficulties. However, causation of the "riots" was in most of these cases complex, and represented a combination of many factor rather than any

Appendix 1. The Special Training Program

single predominate influence. Some were due to organizational problems, living conditions, lack of advancement; others were due largely to social conditions and limitation in work assignments; still others were due to the attitudes shown by white personnel in their objections to Negro personnel intermingling with the local populace, and so forth. The outstanding cases which illustrate this argument show both cause and effect of these attitudes.

APPENDIX 2

A Transcript of the Minutes of the Reunion of Band Members of Great Lakes Naval Training Center, Southern Illinois University, Carbondale, Illinois, Spring 1973

Ladies and gentlemen, welcome to the reunion of the Great Lakes Black Navy Veterans of World War II. The subject or title of this great presentation will be We as the People. Just a small reminder of where we were and where we are now. History tells us that we as a people were the inventors, innovators in the perennial exponent of this type of music called jazz, swing, bop or what have you. As opposed to the European culture or the usual test for music the main difference being melodic, harmonic and rhythmic continuity with a plus and gentlemen and ladies, this is a plus. A real biggy—improvisation. That's the name of the game—improvisation. To recite, sing, oppose or execute anything extemporaneously, but we as a people no longer are leaders, inventors, or innovators of the music of today. Instead, we as a people are followers, imitators and the last decade we are following this interpretation or improvisation of noted harmony and rhythm. By the note and not from our soul. And as a closing statement I would like to relay a quotation I heard in a bar. I know everybody has visited a bar at some time or another where you will always find three or four loud mouths that can expand with great expertise on any subject, any current subject, religion, sports, sex, economy and especially music. This quotation sums up the intelligence of our music by the participating orders of today. And the quote is, 'Who is to say that Beethoven was greater than James Brown?'"

The Saga of Black Navy Veterans of World War II

"My name is Russell Bowman. As we were driving up here today and we said we wonder what the fellows are doing. We have guys in the educational field and all sorts of professions. We know that one of the fellows is marketing signs. We were trying to figure how eight or ten were involved in it. We said 'are there any ministers that we know of in the group? So we said, no, we couldn't think of any ministers. We must have done some mighty bad things. And the Lord hadn't seen anything. Fortunately we do have a member in Chicago. His name is Anderson, Reverend Anderson. I found this in trying to locate Lou Alfred, Pete. Anderson gave me Owsley; that's who I found out we were fortunate to have across the bar."

David Brown: "Speaking of ministers, I just found out today one of our guys is. He is Judd Robertson."

"Our next joyship is named Howard Thunderburg."

"I don't know nothing that I can say other than I'm so glad to be here. I don't want to do nothing, know nothing, absolutely nothing. You know my life is ending but the activity has been all over."

"And the next is a very good friend of mine; a good friend of all of us. We used to work at the post office together; the same unit and the fellows are still questioning why we made this trip here. Our next speaker shall be Mr. Walter Mines."

"I'm not a minister. The closest I've come to being a minister was once. I'm in the purchasing department at Southern University. In attending a purchasing meeting once a fellow came up to me and they needed someone to say grace before the luncheon; just like we are here now, and he didn't know how to ask me about it so one of the fellows come up and asked me: he said, 'Say man, have you ever done any preaching?' I said, 'No, I haven't.' I said, 'what is your problem?' And he said, 'We need somebody to bless the food.' So they officially got somebody, one of the other fellows, I think he

Appendix 2. Reunion of the Band Members

was a fellow from Alexandria, he blessed the food. I want to say that I am very happy to be here. I am sorry that Huel Perkins was not able to come with me this time as usual. He sends his regrets. He knows he's going to regret not being here, but unfortunately there was something else that predated this meeting. He had made a commitment with the school for the government and it didn't come through in time for him to tell anybody he couldn't make it. Yesterday they called him to say that he didn't have to come, but it was too late for him to change his mind because he has to make another trip next week, so that's why he's not here. There was another gentleman who was supposed to come; I don't know if all of you remember his name was Richard Hale. Now Hale lives in Baton Rouge and he was supposed to come but he had something happen to him so he couldn't come, but I'm. here to represent the Baton Rouge fellows, so again I'm happy to be here. Thank you very much."

"Now the next shipmate, we all know him. All the fellows from around St. Louis, and quite a few of us worked with this brother's band for many years. I'd like to present him now: Mr. Charles Williams."

"I want to thank you very much for the little introduction and everything. And shipmates I'm glad to be here with you this year, hope we can make it next year; year after next, and speaking of post office this old man is retired. I enjoy fiddling around every now and then; a little session, try to keep my chops in slip trim, hope we can make it next year and year after next and all the rest of them. Thank you very much."

C. E. Pittman: "One of the things I need to do is make an explanation on starting out from Japs on Stoddard Street. It's been so long since anybody mentioned Stoddard Street, that most of us forgot that street existed. We've run out of where they started, you know and so you can remember that. The middle name Earl came about with Jedd Jellon. Went down and he asked me what my name was and I said, "Corneilious Earl Pittman." And he said, "No, no forget about that Corneilious Earl and have a nice time, you take that to summer school," he said, "and we'll just use the Earl." So it's been Earl Pittman and it's been kind of fortunate to have that name, we have worked a lot of places. I have had the good fortune to work in the school system; the school system of Oklahoma City going on 42 years now. I have had the good fortune of being the public mayor. I know Jimmy Nelson, a very fine musician, and many others including Jack Washington. In Oklahoma City if you say anything about music you ask what about the Willow Brothers? I didn't know these fellows were so well known until I got to Oklahoma, but these fellows had a terrific influence like many musicians. When I see Miss Trump over there it reminds me that I first saw her in Oklahoma City. I was on my first job when I first met that young lady, a fine musician. If you look over there you'll see a very talented young musician, and she can tell you that I've got hundreds of other people out there. The influence of Mrs. Zeila Brough, Dr. Edmund Brough, in the plans from President Lincoln at Wesley. Down through Oklahoma and around the country. To come back and meet with all of you and say a few good things about my good fortune of being a musician, starting with Mrs. Brough. Thank you for inviting me to come back."

"This next person occupies a special place in my heart. When I was sent out to Nebraska I met this little fellow when he was only about eighteen years old, very inexperienced. He was just a nice little fellow. He's a very good trumpet player now. He's a very good friend of mine. He was called Vaughns but his family name is Mason Prince."

"Thank you Frank. I am very fortunate attend the last

Appendix 2. Reunion of the Band Members

reunion we had a few years ago and very, very fortunate to attend this one."

"All right, this next gentleman I don't think was a part of the Great Lakes experience, he's a guest of Mr. Mason Prince, Howard Miller."

"Thank you Mr. Chairman. Would it be too much if I mentioned Army? This is inspiring me to try to do the same thing with our group."

"And our next person I remember very well. Mr. Julius Poole."

"Thank you Mr. Chairman. I hope that you won't forget me in the near future."

"And the next gentleman..."

"Mr. Chairman I was inducted in the Navy as a musician. This is my bag. So I did it at least three years. I still appreciate the fox, note I don't play no music."

"This next gentleman is a very dear, dear friend of mine for forty years I guess. Section base in the band and section base in the Great Lakes band and we're still very dear friends. Meril Tie."

"Thank you. It's good being here and I'm glad to be here for Mr. Bowzer's 75th anniversary. Hope you have some more, hear?"

"I'm just having so much fun. I've been looking forward to it all week, all year and I know that when we left here last year the first thing I did was take my book from 1975 and marked out this weekend. Anybody can call about anything. Just kind of surprised me a little bit that the rest of the guys don't feel that way about this because to me it's very important. I happen to be in sort of a unique situation in that I get around and I see most of the guys around the country and a lot of them have promised me that they were going to show up at Great Lakes and they're not here and Lamont tells me that a lot of them have paid their money and they are coming. I will say that aside from the fact that I get around to see a lot of the guys across the country and around the world, different parts of the world, too. There's a captain here who really makes it his business to keep everybody in touch with everybody else. And I think that is fantastic. Just because it's the university's money...Hey man, have you heard from old so and so. He was hoping we'd call him up and he'd say hey, man I heard from old so and so and he keeps everybody connected. I'd like to also say that Mr. and Mrs. Herman Belle are here. That's my guests and Herman, in fact he's a musician, I'm sure all of you remember him from last year and if he'd of had any choice about it he would have been or actually remembered the Great Lakes experience because he wanted to be in Great Lakes but Uncle Sam wouldn't let him go back and change his mind. But that's Mrs. and Mrs. Herman Belle right there. Thank you."

"Our speaker mentioned that we have a few preachers and reverends and I want you to know that some of my relatives refer to him as the prophet. Also, I remember that in case you weren't aware of it Beethoven was one of us. Okay, we'll talk about that later but just in case you want to remember I just wanted to say it for the record. And the other thing that I wanted to do before sitting down and not taking up too much time as I mentioned to Dr. Floyd Hill. I have a proposal now I'd like to sort of make because I believe this is far too important a thing to be taken short of by those of us who were part of the Great Lakes experience. I think that and I suggested that I've delegated myself to be responsible for a certain area and I think that all here right now should assume the responsibility or be delegated to be responsible for certain territories, certain states, certain city or whatever's close to you, if you want to split it up between two guys. I'm responsible for New York and I should know where I am. Simms, other people, so

Appendix 2. Reunion of the Band Members

on and so forth are not here. I should know if they're going to come, make sure that their bread is here, reservations are made, and if they're not going to show up I should know why. I should be as responsible to him, for that state or that territory then why they say I wonder what's happened to old so and so. You know I can tell you where old so and so is. He's just jive, he don't want to shake. It sounds like a good' thing. I think that would be a good thing for us to do, sort of stick around before we leave here tomorrow and just volunteer to be responsible for certain territories, certain states. I think me and Herman would be happy to represent Missouri or Kansas or both states as he's in that area. At least we would know where all the people are. It would be a good project for us to work on through the years and it would be kind of fun you know, even as much as I trek around the world I would never think myself too busy to bring a full report home. Why these cats not here and who's coming. So I think in the future if we do that we should have a much better turn out. And make it our responsibility to make sure that we coax some of these cats to come; cats who say 'Oh, man, oh, come on.'"

"Thank you. I'm very happy to be here and I'm looking forward to coming back next year, and the year after and many, many years to come."

"By the way, that's one of the best friends I've ever had in my life. You can depend on him for anything. And our next shipmate is Stanley Palace."

"Well the first thing I remember that I was sent to Hampton Institute some of you might remember, and that after about eighteen months or twenty we came back and then we went to Nathan School, Washington, D.C. the same two guys plus Nick Luthsmall, Jack Relionzak, and Dennis Suprenaunt, by the way has anybody ever heard about him? Dennis Suprenaunt, Virgin Islands, St. Thomas? (New York). Anyway, for the last twenty seven years I made set. I've got a small town barn right there about fifty miles south of here; a little town they call Nylons. If you wonder where Nylons is; some of you guys; remember before the war we used to play a place down there called Southern Night Club? Well, that's where I live, and most of you guys don't you remember? And, as usual it's great to be here; nice to see all the old fellows."

"And our next shipmate shall be Mr. Nelson Bradford.

"Sorry but I wasn't a member."

"Oh! Then Melvin E. Lord, Jr."

"Pleased to have an opportunity to share and renew old acquaintances. The very fine experience in 1973. I am a member of the Chapel Hill Band. I'd like to report at this time that three members of the Chapel Hill Band have recently deceased; Sammy Louis Penning, whom I'm sure most of you knew, Harry Curtis, and James Lightfoot. They're all from Washington, D.C. I felt that this might be the opportunity to tell you."

First of all, sincerely, and this is one of the highlights of my life after my wife and I decided that we would attend. I have been like a nervous wreck waiting for the event to come and have really been looking forward to seeing some of the people that I haven't seen for thirty years. I see Clark periodically. We both being in the same business of rat racing around the world and I run into Clark quite often. Most of the guys I haven't seen since the days that I was at Great Lakes and I'd like to commend Dr. Floyd for initiating this get together. It's really a beautiful thing and I'd like to go along with having territorial rights. For instance several people today have asked me about Clarence Francois. I talked to Francois less than two weeks ago and Francois, I think, is familiar with the Chapel Hill Band and I could just as easily have picked him up and brought him here today, but it just, you know, it didn't occur to me to go and

Appendix 2. Reunion of the Band Members

get Francois. So he would have been happy to be here. So on a little resume of my life I've started a second family I have five grandchildren, older than these two. I run into Huel occasionally. The biggest thing in my life now, the biggest asset in life is everything. This is my biggest thing when I go about doing age 55."

"The next shipmate to speak to you is a very, very dear friend of all of us, a hell of a bass player, and a hell of a friend and comedian Major Holyhue!"

"Thank you very much. Move me up to that doctorial salary, your regentship! Of course, naturally it is a great pleasure for me to be here. The decision of trying to come when it is important is partly due to why I am here. However, it was a decision to try to make it to come here, not because I didn't want to be here, because I couldn't afford to much. The purpose is that each time that I've thought about coming something else seems to come up, always. I don't know why but it does. But the importance of being able to see all of the fellows; however, as I look back at going into the Navy, I went in as an apprentice seaman. I was all set to go to Virginia to the machinist school and I saw this young man about two weeks earlier in Denver, Charles Burrell, you may know him. And we had a little get together and through him I think is the reason I got in the band. As a violinist I don't know because I wasn't a very good violin player, I'm still not; however, he was my forerunner to help me get into the band. Now here I am in all this heavy company scraping away on a little bit of violin, I couldn't allude to anything that had to do with music but a little boogey, woogey in the hall way. But in some kind of way that helped me because determination, and what you people have been talking about, determinant attitudes in trying to play some kind of music. For me, I finally found through the Navy music experience as you call it, I don't call it experience because I'm still doing it, it's not experience, it's doing. I'm playing right now. Retirement was forced on me early in life. Now I'm starting to implement all the things I learned up there at Great Lakes, because I didn't play the bass, I didn't know too much about music and through this I've enjoyed some of the happiest times as I've tried to explain to Booty Wood here that I am busy. And it's true, I haven't had this kind of thing happen to me. I'm doing everything; I'm making movies; I'm doing bicentennial things; I've recorded, I've done all kinds of things. In fact listen for a record while you hear the music singing. I am more than appreciative for this whole thing because it has gone about my life, stupid as it is, to be a bass player. Wish all bass players could look like me, pointy head, strong back and bad feet. But it is true, I'm enjoying this whole thing and it is only true since 1942 when I got up to Great Lakes that this happened to me. Now, I'd like to say a few words about the thing about getting the fellows together, I see Skeeter Pest almost constantly. When I go home to Detroit I see people like Billy Homer, a few others; I didn't know Sam Jones was a Navy man; but I think it is a reason why they think that they didn't spend enough time up at Great Lakes. Now I was lucky, as I said I don't know that they stayed up there, bunch of banjo players and all that business. They stayed a few weeks or maybe a few months and then they were sent out somewhere so they don't feel that they are part of this experience because all the ships' company musicians were involved in this. So I think maybe that there should be a point of clearing that particular part up, that all musicians have something to do with playing in the Navy bands. And I agree with Parker, I accept the fact that I don't know nothing about no islands. I'll take Dr. Floyd's contribution to the Navy auditorium. Thank you so much. It's good seeing you all and I hope that is; well first we have to clear up

Appendix 2. Reunion of the Band Members

on that. That Illinois has got to go! I'm talking about Illinois, not the president. I had to really make it here and the people sent me; I ended up in Dupole, Illinois, wherever that is. I got here at 9:25 this morning, in St. Louis, and then I got here around 2:30. Fortunately, I had enough money on the credit card to take care of it. But what I'm talking about, ain't no straight ways to go there. With all that out of the way I am happy to see you all. Thanks."

"This next gentleman has already been introduced, but I think we should hear him say a couple words. Mr. Herman Belle.

"I come from St. Louis. Clark here is really working for us. We're all played together in high school days. Clark wrote me to come to the Navy; I was playing with Jeter Pillar band and I couldn't go. Two days after that the army grabbed me. We referred to him what was happening here, I came; I was here last time and I'll be here every time they have it from now on."

"Well, it's a real pleasure being here. I'm sorry that all of the fellows couldn't make it. As they made it last time, it is really nice and it's nice this time. I just hope there will be more times that we can get together and talk over old times. So let's try and come back again as often as possible. Thanks again."

"Now we shall hear from Mr. Rufus Tucker."

"Mr. Chairman and my fellow shipmates. If you are as accustomed as I am to speaking; just get up, open your mouth and sit down. I'm going to take his advice tonight. I came this time because last time there were more here. I don't see why all the guys couldn't show up because when I learned that they were going to have this reunion I called up every man I knew, California, New York, Hawaii. So I think that we ought to take advantage of these things. And I'll tell you a little history about me getting into the Navy. I guess I was the oldest, so I wasn't thinking we were going to war. The commander I was working under was a reserve officer so he said, 'The Navy's going to get up a Black band and if I were you I would try to get in.' I said, 'Man, I can't get in an all Black band.' He said, 'I think you can.' So I called up every kid that I knew. I said they're going to recruit an all Black band; I said recruit them right here and now so they go down to the post office. So when I got home that night I had a letter right in the mailbox from the recruiter. I ran back up to the post office. He scratched out somebody's name. So now I want to congratulate Mr. Bowzer for doing me a favor. When we came back to the Lakes they split the band up and he said, 'You'll play jazz.' I said, 'I don't want to play jazz. How do you get in the Navy?' So I took the gold metal band and I set it in the water bucket in the washroom. We had washrooms back then. I practiced like mad. And I want to thank him again because when I started teaching that's what I had to teach. So I'm glad especially tonight. And I've also retired. Thank you for letting me sit down a little."

"My name is Charles Burrell from Washington and I was with the band that went to Shoemaker, California. And we were all kids and we didn't know anything or know too much but it was a heck of an experience and I learned quite a bit about being associated with some of the other guys in the other bands like St. Mary's Streetlight, Marshall Hall, George Matthew. Bledsoe, he was over at the base. And all I can say is, man, I sure thank those guys for taking me in then with them so now I am still playing a little bit, but I'm working for the government. So I think this is a nice experience, I'm glad to be here. I hope that I'll be able to come back again."

I'd like to mention two things. One is the value of this type of friendship and comradeship and down in New Orleans attending a meeting connected with the central conference and I'd just come out of a session doing paperwork then. 'What are

Appendix 2. Reunion of the Band Members

you doing?' I said, 'I'm down in a meeting, how long are you going to be there?' 'Leave about 11:37.' He said, 'Are you going straight back?' I said, 'Well, yeah, I guess so.' 'Look here, which way you going?' So we made the arrangement to meet in Hammond. The guy that called me is Walter Mines. Clark said, 'He's spending the university's money.' We left about a half hour later. So when we got back to the Holiday Inn at Hammond, Louisiana, there was Walter Mines and Huel Perkins. So we had this buffet and sat and talked, thinking about the drive thinking about what we were going to do. So they showed us how to get out of Hammond. How to get back on Route 55 going to Boston and to Jackson, Mississippi."

"And now Mr. French."

"Well I feel honored to be here. I appreciate Dr. Floyd asking me to come out. Enough has not been said about his contribution. Maybe they'll be said later, I don't know, but I am honored just to have him part of it. It's been a pleasure for me to meet all of the people that I've met and to just listen to you talk. There is a tremendous amount of history and things that are very important that need to be told to the rest of the world just right in this room. And I hope somebody, some writer or somebody will take it upon themselves to write down some of the important things that we've said about the Great Lakes experience. Again, I'd just like to thank you for allowing me to come in and listen."

"Now we come to the main cog in the wheel of the Great Lakes Experience. Mr. Ed Boggs."

"I've looked forward to this since year before last. It doesn't seem like it's been that long, but please believe me there are two individuals who really catch hell about using too much of Mr. Belle's time and service. Dr. Floyd and yours truly. If he gets an idea about this, there's no end to the time. If I get an idea, I will call him, no end to the time. And we forget to realize that there are other people in our lives that are equally as interested in what we are attempting to do, but they have their hands on time. Get off of that phone! Get off of that phone, you're talking too much and saying nothing. They don't dig what we know because they're not hip to our jive. Now in the kitchen they're the bosses, but when they come to this mess that we're talking about, their boots are not laced. And they're not there long enough to hear the end of the conversation so we can lace their boots and tie them. All they're interested in is get off of that phone, you and Mr. Belle. But they're beautiful people. Get it done! Get it done! Get it done! I don't see how you get so much done in such a short period of time and they're well organized. So when I go back and think of the power that landed through them, I must say we should give Mrs. Floyd a big hand."

"Of course, I'll tell Mrs. Boggs this. These are a few facts that are closest to my heart and I must say this now because it is later than you think. I believe I've got my cards. I believe you've got your cards and of all the cards that I sent out, every name on the list, I wrote the cards, only one came back; that was from Luther Guiness. Last time he was in transit to the west coast, I sent the card to the west coast instead of sending it to New York. He wasn't there. Only one card came back. I'm sure everybody got there cards to find out about the old fox and what was happening. The idea came; Dr. Floyd called and said, 'Nothing's happening man.' I said, 'What's wrong?' He said, 'The guys are not responding.' He said, 'Read it again, I'll make up again.' I called him back and told him about the Guiness and he said, 'Yup! That'll do it.' Then I went down and got post cards and then I had to write this and believe you me, it took a whole lot of time. I had orders not to say that I'm 76. You're not 75, I said, 'You look it.' So I did it anyway because she didn't see the cards. You got the cards. I'm happy

Appendix 2. Reunion of the Band Members

to know that you got the cards because many of you had mentioned it. This is what I'd like to say. I don't know what this is, but it's a lot of stuff, but I think that it is not how you begin a project but how you finish that spells success."

"Beyond any question of doubt, in my opinion those two or three years at Great Lakes was a tremendous success. This occasion is another project of Dr. Floyd's who appreciates your efforts. You would be surprised that this guy says, 'I'll help you, I'll help you.' In the library he was reading about how many guys had stolen our music. That's what he was doing. Do you know so and, so and so. Then we'd get together. They know all of those names because they had such tremendous army bands then and according to this research those bands topped everything in the world. France went for no end. Fortunately for us, this guy here is responsible for us being here. It was his research that produced the bands this time. The army didn't. So here we are in an area district for which we should be proud. I could go ahead and rant and rave about this, but I won't. Have I said enough? This occasion is proof of that ability which depicts the spirit of oneness of purpose, oneness of thought and oneness of action. This is action personified. He has been selected by the men who are responsible for this occasion. For mutual fellowship which is being projected to the world as the Great Lakes Experience. Now I'm told through Dr. Floyd just recently that the town people get it, they want everything, pictures and all of that of this session that some time the most prejudice paper in Chicago, the oldest paper around, the Chicago Tribune, Ebony, everybody wants some of this action now. I was over to Mr. Keller's Tuesday night thinking about Basie and Calloway, Jerome Calloway was there and said, 'This is your band this week.' I said, 'Yes, how do you know?' He said, 'We talked about it in October.' And I'm hip to what's happening. I don't know whether this means as much to you as it means to me. I don't see how it couldn't because I was on the beginning of this. I didn't see how it was done but the people behind me were big people. How the heck those people became interested in what I was able to do God only knows. I'm not a preaching man but I know some bible. I mean I know some bible to the extent of knowing the chapters: Genesis, Exodus, Leviticus, Numbers, Joshua. Everybody will think I'm a preacher. Another thing about that book you talking there is one word to me; just one word, the most powerful word in the bible, and that is the fifth word in the bible. What is it? In the beginning God CREATED. That to me is the greatest word in Webster. Creation. Because you are sinning your inner self to those who follow for tomorrow's usage. Now I'm not a preacher but I can help save your soul. I did help save as I said many a soul. You would be surprised to know that there were more than five thousand musicians who passed through Great Lakes during their tour of duty that I had two places. Sure I heard, and still at my age, Monday night when one called he said, "Man, I hated your guts." He used all of the language of the street to talk about yours truly because he didn't go in with the original 17. They found out there was a band to came back to St. Louis and he wanted to be in that band, he and Eddy Wilkins and all that group delayed their stay to get in that group so they could come back home. When he got there though, he said it isn't the same. But he didn't know I knew what was going to happen at Great Lakes. For him and for the guys who went to St. Louis, I said, 'You don't want that; that isn't what's happening.' I said, 'You're too much of a gentleman Charles to go in on something like that.' He still said it, see. He still doubted. No, he didn't say it behind my back, he would come to my face. Never heard such language in my life. Talking about to yours truly. He was one of the guys who had the audacity to talk to me face

Appendix 2. Reunion of the Band Members

to face. There was lots of reasons for that. Every night for three months I was going to the plantation sitting on the stand with those guys, jiving. He didn't know I was digging him. Many of the guys didn't know that before they were trying to find if I had dug it. That's why they had gone with the Great Lakes Band. I had dug them on their jobs because I was making the ninth navy district. The first guy to know that—you can't imagine who it was... and so I told Terry about this deal, and he said, 'It can't be true.' I said, 'It is true.' He said, 'No, it can't be true.' And I said, 'Terry, you can't be against St. Louis, right?' And couldn't get gig. I said, 'Come and go with me and I want to see that you will become the top trumpet player in the country. Ten years ahead of everybody else.' He said, 'Pops, you're lying.' I said, 'Come on seek the ways of the Navy can be wise.' Terry was the first musician who knew the facts about Great Lakes and I had been all over the district checking out musicians. But see the reason for that was we were the first in war, the first in peace. We needed a bit of peace. That's why you wanted a gig. Mislead the other guys to all of them? Mislead them? His band was to go to California; my band was to be in Great Lakes, but we couldn't say that so we recruited the guys and they felt that they were going to California. When he cut out, he ran out and recruited the guys in California and as soon as we got in, here comes this big 45 piece band from California all together marching along and all a powerhouse came in. Couldn't anybody go in that band. I was two men short. Parade had 45; he brought 43 in and hoped that he was going to put his finger on the St. Louis guys. But as fate would have it yours truly was in command and I would not stand for the guys to be kicked around at all. So this band got together and out they went; he wanted two guys. He wanted to Piggy; I beg your pardon, Clay Brooks and any other guy to fill that band, so I let him stay out there almost two years before filling that spot, I sent, Clay Brooks and Cambro out there to cover that. So that deal was I did not have the honor of sending that band, 45 piece band, there were two 45 piece bands to be formed aside from the 45 piece band at Camp Smalls. The California band I knew about in front, I knew there would eventually be a Carolina band but I didn't know when that would open because of that prejudice down that side, so that was on the list. We got this mess together and Chief Hopes was the guy in charge of this in the beginning. Chief Hopes. The function of Chief Hopes was to train me the navy way when I got control of the navy thing, that blue jacket, and believe me I don't ever want to see another blue jacket anything. I had to learn that thing word for word from A to N. When I recited that thing Annie Peabody was there. When I recited that thing to Annie Peabody that was it. Chief Hopes was assigned to go to Barber's Point. Excuse me ladies: that skunk tried to tear our band at Great Lakes, from pillows. They were tearing everybody; as a result of it I went to the man. I said, 'Look this guy's going to mess up over here. We have this radio program coming in.' He said, 'Okay, he's your baby. Give him what you think he should have.' And that's how he got his guys and we sent him out and from there on it was peace brother, peace. The only big problem we had was the chow hall. Please, if anybody; we've been trying to locate Trice. If anybody can find Trice, please get the message to me or to Dudley Foster. It is; it has been over a period of 30 years since we were at Great Lakes. God the time is flying; 30 years this month since Great Lakes for me. Now as a result of it when all is said and done. I, yours truly, the old fox am happy for this occasion because would like to see you perpetuate this thing for the sake of your posterity because it's later than you think. I've had my day, you try to have yours."

Appendix 2. Reunion of the Band Members

"Now last, but not least, the organizer, the supreme organizer of the whole evening is Dr. Samuel A. Floyd."

"I'd like to comment on a comment that Major Holland made. The comment about Air Illinois I think is made in the right place and the right time because you're in the presence of one of the biggest stock holders of Air Illinois sitting right over there. Secondly, I'd like to say that although I was not a part of the Great Lakes Experience, I've made myself an honorary member because of the influences in the past. This Great Lakes thing didn't just come to me in the past few years. In the early 1950s when I was in college two of my favorite teachers were Richard Haley and Clarence Trice. That's the first time I heard about the Great Lakes Experience. The next time I heard about it was in the early 1960s when I was a fellow faculty member at Florida A&M University in Tallahassee. When he moved to Illinois it was at that time we got deeper into it, got together with Mr. Moore and finally decided to have a reunion. So I am not new to it. It's been on my mind for a long time. And I feel like I am a part of it although I wasn't there. About future reunions: a couple of people have mentioned the idea. If you are interested, if you let me know I'll be glad to organize another one next year. I think Terry's idea is an excellent one of people taking various territories. I think we can have a very successful reunion next time. So just let me know. I have a few announcements to make. Tomorrow at 10 a.m. the ladies and children are invited to my home for the coffee hour and brunch. My wife has our car here and there are others who have cars that will give you a break from these men and all their stories. Tomorrow evening at 7:30 p.m. Mr. Stokes has asked that you meet at the marquee out front that says, 'Welcome Great Lakes Experience,' to have a group picture made in front of the Marquee. So when we come from the buffalo trough at 7:30 prompt please, yes tomorrow evening let's meet in front of the Marquee for a group picture. And finally, when this will be within the next couple of minutes. I hope you will go get your instruments if you brought them and bring them back for a greeting session after which will follow a jam session until 4 or 5 in the morning. Whenever you decide. Thank you."

"I have one more announcement. If any of you would like to come back next week to the reunion, you are welcome because that's where Clark Terry and Anthony Fambro at the reunion. Would it be possible for you to assign a territory and we will respond to you whether or not we will do this? Yeah, I'd be happy to. I'd prefer volunteers first. Well, let's choose a time to do this. Okay, how about tomorrow. Okay, you let me know tomorrow any territories that are not covered, I'll ask various people. Okay we'll take care of it at the buffalo trow as per Mr. Terry's suggestion. At this time I think it would be fitting for us to give three cheers to Dr. Floyd. FLOYD! FLOYD! FLOYD! What was the name of the singing group — Blue Jackets. They were all from Dayton, Ohio. The Blue Jackets. And I'm still back in Dayton, Ohio. Do you have their individual names? I will try to get that from Houser. We know where Strange is. I'll get the list to Dr. Floyd and he can get it to you."

APPENDIX 3

WORLD WAR II BLACK NAVY VETERANS OF GREAT LAKES: CONSTITUTION, CORRESPONDENCE, PRESS RELEASES, ETC.

THE FORTIETH REUNION

The Saga of Black Navy Veterans of World War II

WORLD WAR II BLACK NAVY VETERANS OF GREAT LAKES CELEBRATION

40th ANNIVERSARY

Co-chairmen:
James S. Peters II, Ph.d.
James T. Howard

August 23, 1982

In commemoration of the 40th anniversary of the Black American's acceptance into the General Service of the United States Navy during World War II, we are holding a reunion of Black World War II Navy men on Friday, September 24, 1982 at the Naval Training Center, Great Lakes, Illinois. It was at Great Lakes where these men were trained. This will be the first reunion ever held.

It will be a significant occasion because it represents our efforts to pay homage to a group of unsung heroes, living and dead, who were trailblazers during a dark period of World War II.

Historically, before President Franklin D. Roosevelt opened General Service to Blacks, there were relegated to non-combat roles, such as officers' cooks and stewards. Beginning with Camp Robert Smalls at Great Lakes, there were special segregated camps for Blacks only. Thousands of Black sailors served their country with honor and distinction "on land and on sea."

In 1945 the Navy became the first branch of the armed services to integrate. This was a milestone in the history of race relations in the United States.

There were approximately 70,000 Black sailors who were trained at the Great Lakes Naval Training Station during World War II. These men were drawn from all over the United States.

We are asking your help in locating these veterans by publicizing this news release.

Thank you for your kind attention to this important matter.

Sincerely,

James T. Howard
Co-chairman

Contact:
James T. Howard
P.O. Box 327
Hyannis, MA 02601

Appendix 3. WW II Black Navy Veterans of Great Lakes Notes

WORLD WAR II BLACK NAVY VETERANS OF GREAT LAKES CELEBRATION
40th ANNIVERSARY

PRESS RELEASE

FOR IMMEDIATE RELEASE   August 23, 1982

ANNOUNCING WORLD WAR II BLACK NAVY VETERANS OF GREAT LAKES 40th ANNIVERSARY CELEBRATION. This first reunion will be held at the Naval Training Center, Great Lakes, Illinois on Friday, September 24, 1982. For registration and information contact James T. Howard before September 9, 1982—address: P.O. Box 327, Hyannis, MA 02601. Telephone (617) 775-5741. We urge all Great Lakes veterans to make every effort to attend this first reunion.

Historically, before President Franklin D. Roosevelt opened General Service to Blacks in the United States Navy in 1942, they were relegated to non-combat roles, such as officers' cooks and stewards. With the Blacks acceptance into the General Service such specialties as quartermasters, signalmen, radiomen, boatswains mates, gunners mates, carpenters mates and many more were opened up to them.

There were approximately 70,000 Black sailors trained in segregated camps at the Great Lakes Naval Training Station, Great Lakes, Illinois. Then in 1945 the Navy became the first branch of the armed services to integrate. This was a milestone in the history of race relations in the United States.

This will be a significant occasion because it represents our efforts to pay homage to a group of unsung heroes, living and dead, who were trailblazers during a dark period of World War II.

Contact:
James T. Howard
P.O. Box 327
Hyannis, MA 02601
Tel.: (617) 775-5741

WORLD WAR II BLACK NAVY VETERANS

OF

GREAT LAKES CELEBRATION

40th ANNIVERSARY SEPTEMBER 24, 1982

NAVAL TRAINING CENTER, GREAT LAKES, ILLINOIS

BANQUET PROGRAM

GREETINGS.................................James T. Howard
　　　　　　　　　　　　　　　　　　　　　Master of Ceremonies

PROCLAMATION from Governor James Thompson,
　　　　Illinois............State Senator, Charles Chew, Jr.

PROCLAMATION from Mayor Jane Byrne, City of Chicago
　　　　　　　　　　　...........Vulcan C. Taylor

MESSAGES...................................Atty. Mark E. Jones

WELCOME ADDRESS FROM THE NAVY...Rear Admiral James H. Flatley,
　　　　　　　　　　　　　　　　III, USN

INTRODUCTIONS OF WORLD WAR II BLACK NAVY VETERANS OF GREAT LAKES
　　　　　　　　　...............James T. Howard

INVOCATION.................................Wyman M. Vaughns

DINNER

INTRODUCTION OF SPEAKER....................James T. Howard

ADDRESS....................................DR. JAMES S. PETERS, II

ANNOUNCEMENTS..................Meeting, Saturday, Sept., 25, 1982
　　　　　　　　　　　　　　　Ambassador East Hotel, 10:00 a.m.

CO-CHAIRMEN..............................JAMES S. PETERS, II, Ph.D.
　　　　　　　　　　　　　　　　　　　　JAMES T. HOWARD

BENEDICTION................................Wyman M. Vaughns

ANCHORS AWEIGH

Appendix 3. WW II Black Navy Veterans of Great Lakes Notes

WORLD WAR II BLACK NAVY VETERANS OF GREAT LAKES

<u>Partial Proceedings of the Organizational Meeting Held at the Ambassador East Hotel, Chicago, Illinois on Saturday, September 25, 1982</u>

There were 44 men who became charter members of the World War II Black Navy Veterans of Great Lakes, the name which was adopted by the body for the organization. The charter members are:

James S. Peters, II, Storrs, CT	James S. Griffin, St. Paul, MN
James M. Matthews, Farrell, PA	Douglas W. Johnson, Delmar, NY
Noble Norman, Chicago, IL	James W. Poole, Laurelton, NY
Theodell Bacon, Chicago, IL	George D. Polk, II, St. Louis, MO
Mark E. Jones, Chicago, IL	Culbreth B. Cook, Cleveland, OH
Carson C. Cook, Chicago, IL	Henry A. Martin, Chicago, IL
Louis C. Johnson, Albany, NY	Clinton Hill, Chicago, IL
Bobby J. Wallace, Boston, MA	Jerome S. Cooper, Washington, DC
Lewis R. Williams, Chicago, IL	James O. Lee, Chicago, IL
Gilbert Derr, Chicago, IL	Arthur M. Bowman, Detroit, MI
Alvin Hayes, Wethersfield, CT	Vulcan E. Taylor, Chicago, IL
Robert W. Lofton, Chicago, IL	James R. Carter, Portland, OR
Spottswood L. Tyree, Great Neck, NY	Robert S. Greer, Detroit, MI
Wyman M. Vaughns, Chicago, IL	Morris L. Roller, Chicago, IL
Kenneth O. Wilson, Baltimore, MD	Harry J. Baker, Marlow Heights, MD
Charles Chew, Jr., Chicago, IL	Cardovus T. Patterson, Gary, IN
James Davis, Detroit, MI	Jesse W. Arbor, Chicago, IL
Vincent C. Stuart, Detroit, MI	Ettson Wilkins, Coraopolis, PA
H. S. Rhoden, Chicago, IL	Vernon Jarrett, Chicago, IL
Bernard J. Irvin, Chicago, IL	Leonard Marshall, Detroit, MI
Clarence N. White, Los Angeles, CA	Lyman T. Johnson, Louisville, KY
William W. Smith, Richmond, VA	James T. Howard, Hyannis, MA

Mark E. Jones suggested: 1. A committee be appointed to find out who were at Great Lakes; 2. A committee be appointed to determine where future conventions should be; 3. Start a history and archives of the Great Lakes sailors.

Mark E. Jones volunteered for the Time and Place Committee and Vernon Jarrett for Oral History.

Nominations were opened and James T. Howard was elected Permanent Chairman for 1982-83.

A motion was approved that the Permanent Chairman appoint the following officers, Recording Secretary, Corresponding Secretary, Treasurer, Parliamentarian, Archivist, Assistant Archivist, Master-at-Arms and Assistant Master-at-Arms.

Appointed to these positions were:

> Recording Secretary - James S. Peters, II
> Corresponding Secretary - Cardovus T. Patterson
> Treasurer - Vulcan E. Taylor
> Parliamentarian - Mark E. Jones
> Archivist - Vernon Jarrett
> Assistant Archivist - Louis C. Johnson
> Photographer - H. S. Rhoden
> Master-at-Arms - Bobby J. Wallace
>
> Assistant Master-at-Arms - Clinton Hill

APPRENTICE SEAMEN AND MEMBERS OF SHIP'S COMPANY
STATIONED AT
CAMPS ROBERT SMALLS (MORROW), LAWRENCE, PORTER AND MOFFETT
GREAT LAKES NAVAL TRAINING STATION, GREAT LAKES, ILLINOIS

PLEASE MAIL BACK THIS FORM, EVEN IF YOU ARE UNABLE TO ATTEND.

Dear Mate:

If you have already sent a form and you have no additional information, ignore this request. Thanks for your needed cooperation.

James T. Howard
Permanent Chairman

TYPE OR PRINT

Shipmate's name

Address

_____

Shipmate's name

Address

_____

Shipmate's name

Address

_____

Shipmate's name

Address

_____

Shipmate's name

Address

_____

Names, addresses and zipcodes of TV and radio stations in your area likely to publicize this reunion.

_____

Please mail to:

CARDOVOUS T. PATTERSON
337 Taney Street

Appendix 3. WW II Black Navy Veterans of Great Lakes Notes

6

CHIEF OF NAVAL OPERATIONS

TO
THE WORLD WAR II BLACK NAVY VETERANS OF GREAT LAKES
ON THE OCCASION OF
YOUR 40TH ANNIVERSARY REUNION

As you gather for the first reunion of the World War II Black Navy Veterans of Great Lakes on your 40th Anniversary, you will undoubtedly experience one of the wonderful aspects of Navy life--the memories all of us share with shipmates and friends over the years. Second only to our personal experiences and our relations with other Navy people are memories of the ships in which we sailed, the ports at which we called and the battles we fought.

I am certain you will notice a great difference between the Great Lakes Naval Training Center of today and that of the Camp Robert Smalls where you answered your call to duty. We have made significant progress in making equal opportunity a part of our day to day lives but it was your contributions which blazed the trail for all to follow. I know more must be done and I assure you that I fully intend to continue to press for additional gains on the positive momentum of the past.

It is impossible for me to express my appreciation to you and the other brave Black Americans who have defended this country so ably. I have tremendous respect and admiration for your spirit, your patriotism, your willingness to sacrifice self for the common good and your marvelous record of service --when the nation called, you were there, and you served well and with distinction.

I am heartened by your efforts to preserve the legacy of your companies through your reunion and through your sharing of experiences and memories of your gallantry. I also appreciate your continued concern for keeping our Navy great during the challenging decade of the 1980s. I welcome your support and knowledgeable assistance in keeping it great.

As Chief of Naval Operations, I am pleased to extend on behalf of your U.S. Navy best wishes for a successful and enjoyable reunion to your members and guests on this your 40th Anniversary. God Bless.

JAMES D. WATKINS
Admiral, U.S. Navy

THE SECRETARY OF DEFENSE
WASHINGTON, D.C. 20301

Mr. James T. Howard 18 August, 1982
P.O. Box 327
Hyannis, MA 02601

Dear Mr. Howard:

Thank you for your letter regarding the first reunion of World War II Black Navy Veterans of Great Lakes.

The 40th Anniversary of your group marks a significant milestone in our nation's history.

I've asked the Secretary of the Navy to provide assistance in arranging the visit to the Great Lakes Naval Training Center on September 25, 1982.

Unfortunately, the demands of my schedule will preclude my attendance. However, please extend my personal best wishes to all in attendance, and accept my salute to each of you as great Americans who answered our nation's call.

Sincerely,

Caspar Weinberger

Appendix 3. WW II Black Navy Veterans of Great Lakes Notes

THE UNDER SECRETARY OF THE NAVY
WASHINGTON D C. 20350

17 August 1982

Mr. James T. Howard
P.O. Box 327
Hyannis, MA 02601

Dear Mr. Howard:

The Secretary of the Navy asked me to respond to your letter of July 23, 1982, regarding the 40th Anniversary of the World War II Black Navy Veterans of Great Lakes.

We agree with you that this first reunion will mark a most significant occasion in American history.

A copy of your letter has been forwarded to the Public Affairs Officer at the Great Lakes Naval Training Center. Lieutenant Commander C. A. Davis, telephone (312) 688-2201, will contact you and make arrangements for your requested visit on Saturday, September 25.

It is regretted that the Secretary's schedule will preclude his attendance at the reunion, but in behalf of the Secretary and myself, please extend our best wishes for a most joyous and memorable reunion.

Sincerely,

JAMES F. GOODRICH

THE SECRETARY OF DEFENSE
WASHINGTON, D.C. 20301

18 AUG 1982

Mr. James T. Howard
P.O. Box 327
Hyannis, MA 02601

Dear Mr. Howard:

    Thank you for your letter regarding the first reunion of World War II Black Navy Veterans of Great Lakes.

    The 40th Anniversary of your group marks a significant milestone in our nation's history.

    I've asked the Secretary of the Navy to provide assistance in arranging the visit to the Great Lakes Naval Training Center on September 25, 1982.

    Unfortunately, the demands of my schedule will preclude my attendance. However, please extend my personal best wishes to all in attendance, and accept my salute to each of you as great Americans who answered our nation's call.

Sincerely,

Caspar W. Weinberger

Appendix 3. WW II Black Navy Veterans of Great Lakes Notes

September 2, 1982

Mr. James T. Howard
P.O. Box 327
Hyannis, MA 02601

Dear Mr. Howard,

    Thank you sincerely for thinking of me in connection with World War II black Navy veterans of the Great Lakes. Regretfully, I am currently committed for that date.

    I also am sorry about the error in reviewing officers. It's been about three years since I've done that, so it's time I do it again. However, as you well know, no one asked me.

    I sincerely hope that all of you thoroughly enjoy the reunion. I am sure it will be a great day.

    Best regards.

                    Sincerely,

                    SAMUEL L. GRAVELY, JR.
                    VADM, U.S.N. (Ret.)

SLG:cwk

STATE OF ILLINOIS
OFFICE OF THE GOVERNOR
SPRINGFIELD 62706

JAMES R. THOMPSON
Governor

September 8, 1982

James S. Peters II, Ph.D.
Chairman
World War II Black Navy Veterans
  of Great Lakes Celebration
P.O. Box 327
Hyannis, Massachusetts 02601

Dear Dr. Peters:

    As Governor of Illinois, I wish to thank you for choosing Illinois and the City of Chicago as the site of your 1982 Convention.

    I'm sure you will not regret this decision. The many conveniences and unending hospitality Chicago possesses will make this event quite memorable for everyone in attendance.

    Please extend my personal welcome to all your members and may your convention be a huge success.

Sincerely,

James R. Thompson
GOVERNOR

JRT:mf

Appendix 3. WW II Black Navy Veterans of Great Lakes Notes

OFFICE OF THE MAYOR
CITY OF CHICAGO

JANE M. BYRNE
MAYOR

September 15, 1982

Mr. James S. Peters, II Ph.D.
Chairman
WORLD WAR II BLACK NAVY VETERANS
OF GREAT LAKES CELEBRATION
P. O. Box 327
Hyannis, MA 02601

Dear Dr. Peters:

As Mayor of the City of Chicago, as well as personally, I am very pleased to extend a cordial welcome to the WORLD WAR II BLACK NAVY VETERANS OF GREAT LAKES CELEBRATION on the occasion of your 1982 convention.

Chicago is proud of its reputation as "Convention Capital of the Nation." We are quite confident that the unparalleled facilities of our city will enhance the success of your meeting bringing about the maximum in attendance.

During the few moments available to you during your business and technical sessions, please be assured that there are many regular and special events in the city for your mutual enjoyment and interest.

We hope your group will return to Chicago many times in the future.

Sincerely,

MAYOR

DEPARTMENT OF THE NAVY
NAVAL TRAINING CENTER
GREAT LAKES, ILLINOIS 60088

FT31-N3/LRC:lo
5720

SEP 14 1982

James T. Howard
P.O. Box 327
Hyannis, MA 02601

Dear Mr. Howard:

We are delighted that you and the many black World War II Navy Veterans have included us in your celebration. It is an honor to have those of you who helped bring about such an important step in the growth of our Navy, and our nation on board the Naval Training Center.

All arrangements have been made for your visit on September 24, 1982. Tables have been reserved for the 40 reunion attendees at the VIP Luncheon. The luncheon begins at 11:30 a.m. It is held at the Consolidated Mess (open) building 140. The meal price of approximately $4.00 per person should be paid at the door. Your group will be recognized as our Special Guest of Honor. They will also be attending the Recruit Graduation Review which follows the luncheon. It begins at 1:30 p.m. and is held at the Recruit Training Command, Gallery Hall. Unfortunately, we will be unable to invite RADM Samuel L. Gravely to be the Reviewing Officer since we already have a Reviewing Officer scheduled for that date. RADM Gravely's address is listed below for your own use:

15956 Waterfall Road
Haymarket, VA 22069

The arrangements for your banquet have also been made. The banquet is scheduled for September 24th in the Harbor Room, Main Floor of the Consolidated Mess (open), building 140. Cocktails will be served beginning at 4:30 p.m. There will be a private, cash bar which will close at 6:00 p.m. and reopen at 7:30 p.m. Dinner will be served at 7:00 p.m.

Since the Naval Training Center is sponsoring your group, the Public Affairs Office has signed the contract. A copy of the contract is attached. Current arrangements call for meals for 50 people. We will need an exact count no later than September 10th. Please forward your check for the cost of the meals to LT(jg) Cantrell prior to the banquet. You will need to contact Mr. George Karas, Manager of the CMO to finalize the details. He can be reached at (312) 688-6946.

RADM Flatley has agreed to speak at the banquet. We have enclosed his biography and picture for your use. Please contact LT Tim Beatty, (312) 688-3400, and let him know what time the Admiral should be at the CMO, how long you would like him to speak and any other instructions he may need.

Appendix 3. WW II Black Navy Veterans of Great Lakes Notes

The Public Affairs Office will be coordinating your visit here. Please feel free to contact LT(jg) Lynn Cantrell if you have any questions or are in need of further assistance.

We look forward to seeing you.

Sincerely,

WILLIAM B. DERMODY
Assistant Public Affairs Officer
By direction of the Commander

Enclosures

THE NATIONAL ENDOWMENT FOR THE ARTS

AND

SOUTHERN ILLINOIS UNIVERSITY AT CARBONDALE

ORAL HISTORY PROJECT

INTERVIEWEES:	Len Bowden (LB) Thomas Bridge (TB) Howard Funderburg (HF) Major Holley (MH) Huel Perkins (HP) Charles Pillars (CP)	Hayes Pillars (HPi) Clark Terry (CT) Rufus Tucker (RT) Ernie Wilkins (EW) Jimmy Wilkins (JW) Mitchell 'Booty' Wood (MW)
MODERATOR:	Samuel A. Floyd, Jr. (SF)	Associate Professor of Music at Southern Illinois University at Carbondale
INTERVIEWERS:	London Branch (LBr)	Director of Jazz Studies at Mississippi Valley State University Itta Bena, Mississippi
	Warrick Carter (WC)	Chairman of the Music Department at Governors State University, Park Forest South, Illinois
SUBJECT:	THE GREAT LAKES EXPERIENCE: 1942-1945	
DATE:	September 9, 1976	

Any conclusions drawn or implications made do not necessarily represent the view of the endowment.

Appendix 3. WW II Black Navy Veterans of Great Lakes Notes

AFFIDAVIT—ASSOCIATIONS,
CLUBS, ORGANIZATIONS, ETC

TO:

July 18, 1983

I, the undersigned, Secretary of _The World War II, Black Navy Veterans of Great Lakes_ do hereby certify that the following is a complete, true, and correct copy of certain resolutions adopted at a duly called meeting held on the _25th_ day of _September_ 1982 and that said resolutions are set forth in the minutes of said meeting and have not been rescinded or modified.

BE IT RESOLVED, that _The Independent Bank of Chicago_ be and hereby is designated a depository in which the funds of this Organization be deposited by its officers, agents, and employees and each of them hereby is authorized to endorse for deposit or negotiation any and all checks, drafts, notes, bills of exchange, and orders for the payment of money, either belonging to or coming into the possession of this Organization. Endorsements for deposit may be by the written or stamped endorsement of the Organization without designation of the person making the endorsement.

BE IT FURTHER RESOLVED, that any _two_ of the following
James T. Howard, James S. Peters,
Vulcan C. Taylor
are authorized to SIGN ANY AND ALL CHECKS, DRAFTS, AND ORDERS, including orders or directions in informal or letter form, against any funds at any time standing to the credit of this Organization with the said bank, and/or against any account of this Organization with the said Bank, and the said Bank hereby is authorized to honor any and all checks, drafts and orders so signed, including those drawn to the individual order of any such officer and/or other person signing the same, without further inquiry or regard to the authority of said officer(s) and/or other person(s) or the use of said checks, drafts and orders, or the proceeds thereof.

BE IT FURTHER RESOLVED, that each of the foregoing resolutions, directions, and instructions, shall continue in force until express written notice of its recision or modification has been received by the Bank. It is agreed for the purpose of inducing the said Bank to act hereunder that said Bank shall be saved harmless from any loss suffered or liability incurred by it in acting hereunder.

I FURTHER CERTIFY that the following named persons are the officers of the said Organization, duly qualified and now acting as such:

~~President~~ Chairman _James T. Howard_ Asst. Secretary_____
Vice President _____ Asst. Treasurer _____
Secretary _James S. Peters_
Treasurer _Vulcan C. Taylor_

The World War II Black Navy Veterans of Great Lakes
(Name of Organization)

Attest: By _James S. Peters_ _____ Secretary
By _James T. Howard_ Permanent Chairman _____ Retiring Secretary

NEW MAILING ADDRESS_____

THE FORTY-FIRST REUNION

Appendix 3. WW II Black Navy Veterans of Great Lakes Notes

ANNOUNCING

WORLD WAR II BLACK NAVY VETERANS OF GREAT LAKES CELEBRATION

41ST ANNIVERSARY

CELEBRATION - 41st Anniversary Reunion
    Naval Training Center
    Great Lakes, Illinois

JUST COME ON!

SCHEDULE OF EVENTS

__Thursday Evening, August 25, 1983__
    Hyde Park Hilton Inn, Chicago, Illinois
    Get Together - Suite 438 --- 7:00 P.M.

__Friday, August 26, 1983__
    Naval Training Center, Great Lakes, Illinois -- Bus leaves Hotel at 9:30 Sharp.

1130 hours VIP Luncheon (dutch treat, $4.00) as the guest of Commodor Thomas Emery, Commandant of the Naval Training Center at the Consolidated Mess (open), Building 140.

1330 hours Recruit Graduation R-view. Held at the Recruit Training Command, Gallery Hall.

1600 hours Cocktail Party at the Consolidated Mess (open), Building 140. Cash bar, drinks 95¢, top shelf $1.50.

1800 hours Banquet at the Consolidated mess (open), Bu8lding 140. Cost of the banquet included in the Registration Fee.

__Saturday, August 27, 1983__
    Hyde Hilton Inn, Chicago, Illinois
    10:00 A.M. World War II Black Navy Veberans of Great Lakes meeting
    Afternoon - Open
    There is a beach and swimming in Lake Michigan across from the hotel. Also pool. There are pretty women in teeny-weeny bikinis lying around on the beach -- There is bus transporation to center city Chicago where there is fabulous shopping for your wife, while you are on the beach looking.

WORLD WAR II BLACK NAVY VETERANS OF GREAT LAKES

May 30, 1983

Mr. Mark E. Jones, Esq.
Parliamentarian
Lafonte, Wilkins and Jones
Suite 1423-Brunswick Building
69 Washington Street
Chicago, IL 60602

Dear Mark:

The time is rolling around again for the reunion of the World War II Black Navy Veterans of Great Lakes. It is tentatively scheduled for August 25-27, 1983 with the Hyde Park Hilton in Chicago as our headquarters. We have asked permission to hold our celebration at Great Lakes again on Friday August 26. So far we have had no reply from the Navy and that is our holdup.

However, at the meeting last year at the Ambassador East Hotel, you were elected parliamentarian. You also volunteered to write a constitution. I sincerely hope that you will have time to do so by the time of our 41st Anniversary reunion.

Some of the items which you might consider to be included would be the officers, their duties and terms. At present the officers are: permanent chairman, vice chairman, recording secretary, corresponding secretary, treasurer, parliamentarian, archivist, master-at-arms and assistant master-at-arms. How about standing committees, such as time and place and membership? The membership committee's duties could include your suggestion about finding out who were at Great Lakes, for that is what they are really doing now as well as getting members for our organization. You could look at my title of permanent chairman. I really do not believe that anyone last year gave serious thought to making me chairman in perpetuity. Maybe there should be some different titles.

You also volunteered for the Time and Place Committee. I apprised Wyman Vaughns of that fact and I hope that you will get in touch with him and lend him a hand. His address is 6812 Cornell Avenue, Chicago, IL 60649 and his telephone number is 752-7853. The other members of the committee are: Lewis (Mummy) Williams, Vernon Jarrett and Vulcan Taylor.

Please let me hear from you.

Sincerely,

James T. Howard
Permanent Chairman
P.O. Box 327
Hyannis, MA 02601
Telephone: (617) 775-5741

cc: Wyman Vaughns

Appendix 3. WW II Black Navy Veterans of Great Lakes Notes

WORLD WAR II BLACK NAVY VETERANS OF GREAT LAKES

August 2, 1983

Mr. William Williams
Director of Sales
Chicago Convention and Tourist Bureau
McCormick Place on the Lake
Chicago, IL 60616

Dear Bill:

    The World War II Black Navy Veterans of Great Lakes is having its 41st Anniversary Reunion in Chicago and at Great Lakes August 25-27, 1983. Our headquarters will be the Hyde Park Hilton Inn, 4900 So. Lake Shore Drive, Chicago. I wonder if you could, with even this short notice, obtain for us greetings or a proclamation from Mayor Harold Washington and Governor Thompson of Illinois? I am asking Lewis R. (Mummy) Williams to be the contact person for you. His address is, 1728 East 92nd Place, Chicago, IL 60617. His telephone number is 768-2466.

    We really appreciate your getting the proclamations from Mayor Jane Byrne and Governor Thompson last year. Thank you so much.

    The Black Navy Veterans really enjoyed coming back to Chicago and Great Lakes last year, so much so that it was decided to have our reunion there again this year.

    Enclosed is an announcement of the reunion.

                                     Sincerely,

                                     James T. Howard
                                   Permanent Chairman
                                   P. O. Box 327
                                   Hyannis, MA 02601
                                   Tel.: (617) 775-5741

cc: Wyman M. Vaughns, Black Navy Veterans
    James S. Peters, II, Black Navy Veterans
    Lewis R. Williams, Black Navy Veterans
    Charles Chew, Black Navy Veterans

Enclosure

The Saga of Black Navy Veterans of World War II

WORLD WAR II BLACK NAVY VETERANS OF GREAT LAKES

August 17, 1983.

LTjg Paul Owens
Public Affairs Officer
Great Lakes, IL 60088

Dear LT Owens:

    The World War II Black Navy Veterans of Great Lakes is having its 41st Anniversary Reunion in Chicago and at Great Lakes August 25-27, 1983. This is an organization whose members are those Black sailors who were trained at Great Lakes during World War II. Before 1942 the Blacks were limited mainly to the stewards mates branch. One of our purposes is to recruit minorities for the Navy.

    We are having our cocktail party (cash bar) and banquet at the CMO, Naval Training Center, Great Lakes on Friday, August 26, 1983. The cocktail party is at 1600 and the banquet is at 1800. The cost of the banquet for the Black officers and wives is $12.95 per person.

    Last year LT Gerald Collins had asked if the black officers at NTC could come to our banquet and they did. It was a great experience to mingle with them. I am asking you to spread the word that they are welcome again this year.

    Incidentally, Nathan Penn is a member of our organization. Looking forward to meeting you.

    We need a count.

                                            Sincerely,

                                            James T. Howard
                                            Permanent Chairman

Please Address Reply To:
    James T. Howard
    P. O. Box 327, Hyannis, MA 02601
    Telephone: (617) 775-5741

From August 24-28, 1983
    Hyde Park Hilton Inn
    4900 South Lake Shore Drive
    Chicago, IL 60615
    Telephone: (312) 288-5800

cc: Wyman M. Vaughns, Black Navy Veterans
    James S. Peters, II, Black Navy Veterans

Appendix 3. WW II Black Navy Veterans of Great Lakes Notes

WORLD WAR II BLACK NAVY VETERANS OF GREAT LAKES

August 9, 1983

Mr. Mark E. Jones
LaFontant, Wilkins, Jones & Ware
Suite 1423 - Brunswick Building
69 West Washington Street
Chicago, IL 60602

Dear Mark:

That was a very wonderful job which you did on the constitution. That should put us in business.

There were several small changes and one addition which I have to suggest:

1. The name of the organization should be World War II Black Navy Veterans of Great Lakes, which was the one which was adopted at the meeting last year. The other name would probably be too inclusive. It would take in stewards mates, who trained in a number of places, the Seabees who trained at Camp Peary, Virginia and the like.

2. Maybe we ought to retain Master of Arms instead of Sergeant at Arms for the naval flavor as we had this year.

How about the signing of the checks? Two out of three officers? President, Secretary and Treasurer? Right now we are doing it that way, me as chairman, Vulcan Taylor as treasurer and Jim Peters as secretary.

I contacted Judge Parsons to have him as our main speaker. He called me to say that he would let me know in a few days if he would be free to do it. I have not heard from him since. I am assuming that he probably will do that for us. Mummy Williams, Wyman Vaughns suggested him.

Have a good vacation. Thanks for a job well done.

Sincerely,

James T. Howard
Permanent Chairman
P.O. Box 327
Hyannis, MA 02601
Tel.: (617) 775-5741

cc: James S. Peters, II

WORLD WAR II BLACK NAVY VETERANS OF GREAT LAKES

August 10, 1983

Mr. Mark E. Jones, Esq.
Lafontant, Wilkins, Jones & Ware
Suite 1423 - Brunswick Building
69 West Washington Street
Chicago, IL 60602

Dear Mark:

    I am sorry that I did not include these items in my letter of yesterday (August 9, 1983) and I hope that it will not mess up your schedule too much.

1. Article IV, on page 2, --- at one time or another during World War II. Instead of World War II, I think it should be, June 1942 through August 1945. This was adopted at the meeting last year.

2. Maybe we need mention of some provision for starting chapters around the country. - There is a group in the New York area which has been meeting recently. One of their purposes would be fund raising to send shipmates to our conventions who would not be able to afford it. - A California group had been meeting for a number of years. However, I was unable to make contact with any of them. - Some musicians have been convening every year.

I hope that you can incorporate these items.

                              Sincerely,

                              James T. Howard
                              Permanent Chairman
                              P.O. Box 327
                              Hyannis, MA 02601
                              Tel.: (617) 775-5741

cc: James S. Peters, II

Appendix 3. WW II Black Navy Veterans of Great Lakes Notes

CONSTITUTION OF THE BLACK NAVY VETERANS
OF WORLD WAR II

ARTICLE I: NAME OF ORGANIZATION

The name of this Illinois Not-For-Profit Corporation shall be the WORLD WAR II BLACK NAVY VETERANS OF GREAT LAKES (adopted at the meeting - hereafter called **ORGANIZATION**).

ARTICLE II: Purpose

Purposes of the **ORGANIZATION** are:

A. To continue the fellowship commenced during our war time activities at Great Lakes and at other Naval Stations throughout the world.

B. To foster and encourage a feeling of good will among Black youth for the United States Navy with a view to encouraging them to enlist and to take advantage of the many opportunities it affords.

C.

D.

ARTICLE III: Office

The Corporation shall have and maintain a registered office which address shall be in the city of _____, _____.

ARTICLE IV: Membership

Membership in this **ORGANIZATION** shall be open to all United States Navy Veterans who trained and served at Great Lakes Naval

Training Station at one time or another during World War II June 1942-August 1945.

ARTICLE V: Officers

The members of the ORGANIZATION shall, at an Annual Meeting to be held in the month of August of each year, or at such other time as the membership decides to select the following officers: a President, a Vice President, a Secretary, a Corresponding Secretary, a Treasurer, a Parliamentarian, and a Master at Arms.

The members may create and fill any other offices that he deems necessary to carry out the function of its Charter.

ARTICLE VI: Board of Directors

The ORGANIZATION shall select a Board of Directors.

The Board of Directors of the ORGANIZATION shall consist of the elected officers and four (4) additional persons to be chosen by the members at the Annual Meeting. Directors' terms shall be for two (2) years, with two (2) Directors being elected initially for a one (1) year period and two (2) Directors for a two (2) year period.

ARTICLE VII: Duties of the Board

The Board shall exercise all corporate powers and implement policies and programs decided on by the members. They shall meet from time to time, and deal with matters not decided by the members of the Annual Meeting.

ARTICLE VIII: Term of Office of Officers

All officers shall serve in office for one year or until his successor has been elected and qualified.

ARTICLE IX: Vacancies

Any vacancy occurring on the Board by reason of death, resignation or other inability will be filled by the Board of Directors at the earliest opportunity.

ARTICLE X: Meetings

The regular meetings of the Organization will be held each year at a time and place to be designated by the members upon the advice and recommendation of a Time and Place Committee.

Meetings of the Board may be held at such places and at such times as the Board shall decide.

ARTICLE XI: Quorum

One-third (1/3) of the membership of the Organization, or of the Board of Directors shall constitute a Quorum for the transaction of business at any meeting of the Board of the membership.

ARTICLE XII: Notice

Notices of the Annual Meeting and of any special meeting of the ORGANIZATION or of the Board of Directors shall be by mail and shall be supplied to all members in good standing at least thirty (30) days prior to the date of such meeting.

ARTICLE XIII: Removal

Any officer or member of the Board may be removed by a two-thirds (2/3) vote of the Board whenever in its judgment the best interest of the ORGANIZATION would be served thereby. But, such removal shall be after thirty (30) days notice to the person sought to be removed and after an appropriate hearing by the Board.

ARTICLE XIV: Duties

1. Duties of the President.

    The President shall be the principal Executive Officer of the ORGANIZATION and shall supervise and control its business affairs. He shall preside at all meetings of the membership and of the Board, and shall together with the Treasurer or Secretary sign all checks which are authorized by the Board or by the membership.

2. Duties of the Vice President.

    In the absence of the President or in the event of his death or inability to act the Vice President shall perform the duties of the President and when so acting shall have all the powers and duties of the President. The Vice President shall in addition to the above duties, perform such other duties as from time to time may be assigned to him by the President or by the Board of Directors.

3. Secretary.

The Secretary shall keep the Minutes of the meetings of the members and of the Board of Directors in one or more books provided for that purpose; see that all notices are duly given in accordance with the provision of these by-laws, or as are required by law; be custodian of the corporate records and of the Seal of the **ORGANIZATION**, and see that the Seal of the **ORGANIZATION** is affixed where necessary for all official documents.

4. Corresponding Secretary.

The Corresponding Secretary shall handle the general correspondence, including notices of meetings and keep a record of correspondence of other officials. Additionally, the Corresponding Secretary shall provide all members of the **ORGANIZATION** with copies of Minutes of all meetings, motions passed, and the names, addresses and telephone numbers of all members of the **ORGANIZATION**.

5. Treasurer.

If required by the Board of Directors, the Treasurer shall give a bond for the faithful performance of his duties in such sum and with such surety or sureties as the Board of Directors shall determine. He shall have charge of and be custodian of all funds of the **ORGANIZATION**; shall receive and give receipts for monies due and payable to the **ORGANIZATION** from any source whatsoever and deposit all such monies in the name of the ORGANIZATION in such banks, trust companies or other depositories as shall be selected in accordance with direction of the membership or of the Board. He shall additionally, in cooperation with the members of the Board of Directors or with any Finance Committee the membership of the Board establishes, prepare a budget, and shall see to its faithful execution.

ARTICLE XV: Committees

1. Committees of Directors.

   The Board of Directors by resolution adopted by a majority of the Officers and Directors in office may designate an Executive Committee which Committee shall exist of three (3) or more officers or members of the Board. To the extent provided for in the resolution establishing the Executive Committee they shall exercise the authority of the Board in the absence of meeting of the Board. The designation of such Committee and delegation to it of authority shall not, however, operate to relieve the Board of Directors or any individual Director of any responsibility imposed upon him by law or by these by-laws.

2. The President shall appoint any Committee, and designate its Chairman to carry out the requirements, policies or programs of the ORGANIZATION. The Chairman of each Committee must be a member of the ORGANIZATION. The Chairman or any member of any Committee may be removed

by the President whenever in his judgment the best interest of the ORGANIZATION Shall be served by such a move.
4. Standing Committees.
Standing Committees of the ORGANIZATION shall be as follows:
1. Executive Committee.
2. Membership Committee.
3. Program Committee.
4. Finance Committee.
5. Budget Committee.
6. Publicity Committee.
7. Constitution and By-Laws.

ARTICLE XVI: Contracts, Checks, Deposit and Funds
Section 1: Contracts.
The Board of Directors may authorize any officer or agents of the Center in addition to the officers so authorized by these by-laws to enter into any contract or execute and deliver any instrument in the name of and on behalf of this ORGANIZATION.

Section 2: Deposits:
All funds of the ORGANIZATION shall be deposited to the credit of the ORGANIZATION in such banks, trust companies or other depositories as the Board of Directors may select.

Section 3: Dues
The membership from time to time may determine the amount of dues required of each member of the ORGANIZATION.

ARTICLE XVII: Default and Termination of Membership

When any member shall be in default in the payment of dues for more than one month from the beginning of the fiscal year, his membership thereupon may be terminated.

ARTICLE XVIII: Seal

The Board of Directors shall provide a Corporate Seal which shall be in the form of a circle and shall have inscribed thereon the name of the corporation and the words "Corporate Seal."

ARTICLE XIX: Waiver of Notice

Whenever any notice is required to be given under the provisions of the General Not-For-Profit Corporation Act of the State of Illinois or under any other state that this Corporation may become organized, a waiver thereof in writing signed by the person or persons entitled to such notice whether before or after the time stated therein it shall be deemed equivalent to the giving of such notice.

ARTICLE XX: Amendments to The Constitution

This Constitution may be altered, amended or repealed and by-laws may be adopted by a two-thirds (2/3) vote of the members present at any Annual Meeting of the ORGANIZATION, provided that notice of any proposed change or amendment is supplied to the members at least thirty (30) days before the commencement of such meeting.

Appendix 3. WW II Black Navy Veterans of Great Lakes Notes

LOOKING TO THE FUTURE...

WORLD WAR II BLACK NAVY VETERANS OF GREAT LAKES
CHICAGO, ILLINOIS

July 27, 1984

Dear Member of the Executive Committee:

    A matter has come up which, if carried to its completion, would require an expenditure of funds, that is not connected with putting on our 42nd Anniversary Reunion in Chicago.

    Wyman M. Vaughns of Chicago has obtained a list of the June 1984 graduates of Dunbar High School, Chicago, Illinois. They number about 375 and are predominately Black. Dunbar is an elite high school, requiring an entrance examination, therefore these graduates should be a cut above the average high school graduate.

    Jesse W. Arbor, also of Chicago, in line with one of our purposes, which is to recruit minorities for service in the United States Navy, telephoned Commodore T. R. M. Emery, commander of the Naval Training Center, Great Lakes, Illinois and obtained his OK to have the Navy transport between 50 and 75 of these graduates to Great Lakes, give them a tour of the base, lunch and a seat at the Recruit Graduation Review and return them to Chicago. All of this would take place on August 24, 1984 in conjunction with our reunion at Great Lakes. I have written to Commodore Emery to confirm this.

    Should this plan be feasible, it will require expenditures of about $75.00 for postage and about $30.00 for duplicating costs to find out which of these graduates are interested in enlisting in the Navy and who would like a trip to Great Lakes.

    I would appreciate a quick response to this request, so that we can go ahead at a moment's notice.

    Looking forward to seeing you in Chicago for our reunion.

                                  Sincerely yours,

                                  James T. Howard
                                  President

Please address a quick reply to:
James T. Howard
P. O. Box 327, Hyannis, MA 02601
(617) 775-5741

Enclosure

APPENDIX 4

World War II Black Navy Veterans Celebrate the Fiftieth Anniversary of Entrance Into General Service of the U.S. Navy, June 20, 1992: A Transcript of the Minutes

World War II Black Navy Veterans of Great Lakes
Saturday, June 20, 1992
Regency Ballroom, Hyatt Regency, Chicago, Illinois

The Banquet

Guest Speaker: Rear Admiral Mack C. Gaston

President, distinguished guests ladies and gentlemen I am indeed honored with the distinct pleasure of having the opportunity to speak to such a distinguished group this evening; World War II Black Navy Veterans. It is such a distinct pleasure that it's difficult for me to start and I will start by saying this. There's no way Commander Kendall, Captain Womack or for me, Admiral Mack Gaston, to be what we are if it had not been for you. This was my call; paving the way. You suffered through a lot. I don't have to remind you of that, but I just had to say that. You took a lot of stuff. But I want you to know for a solid, good reason, and it's paying off every day. Now I don't mean by that that we don't have problems today. We don't have the same kind, and yes there have been eleven flag officers. And out of that eleven, two have recently been assigned as. three stars so we now have seven three star admirals. Admiral Paul Reason, who is the commander of the service forces, Atlantic fleet, and I think all of us know who the first one was, Admiral Sam Gravely. So there again, I am distinctly honored to have the pleasure to talk to you."

It was a pleasure and also an honor last night to have the opportunity to talk to many of you and tonight before this function started I learned a lot of history. A lot of good stuff that I am going to relay to a lot of people. But after such a kind introduction I am reminded of what President Franklin Roosevelt said to his son James, 'When you speak to the President remember three things: be sincere, be brief and be seated...' But I am also reminded of what the late Prime Minister of Israel, Golda Meir once said, 'Don't be so humble — you're not that great.'"

As I've noted, all of you here are that great and that includes the wives because you fought a war that they fought differently. You supported their efforts and you probably did some things that they couldn't do while they were engaged with the Navy. So you had to carry on and that's still happening today so I think the support of the families is vital to the success of all of us."

I want to talk a little bit about another *kind* of war that we fought. Some people call this the greatest continent of all. You'll probably argue with that, but listen just a moment. I call it the greatest continent of all and we won; I'm talking about the cold war. We have just passed through an era of immense danger, frequently on the brink, of nuclear catastrophe. Have we ever been challenged with a more potentially deadly war, one that even threatens the extinction of the human race? Think about it. Let's hope that the nation will not soon forget the dedication of the soldiers, sailors, marines and airmen who were so diligent in their efforts to keep the peace and win the cold war."

The world should also never forget you World War II

Appendix 4. Notes from the 50th Anniversary Banquet

veterans who gave everything they had and maybe gave the ultimate sacrifice of their lives. I want to take this powerful opportunity to thank you on behalf of the entire nation and the entire world. Give yourselves a hand."

This evening I will talk to you about change. Change in the nuclear community and change in our Navy and how these changes must be coupled with dynamic and continuous leadership. Our world is undergoing many changes. President John F. Kennedy said, 'Change is the law of life and those who look only on the past or the present are certain to miss the future.'"

The defense nuclear agency is working hard to keep pace with these changing events in the nuclear community. As was stated by Captain Womack at the introduction, I am the commander of the defense nuclear agency field command the operating arm of the defense nuclear agency, so let me tell you a little bit of the how the field command fits into this nuclear community. We first become involved with nuclear weapons designed early in the development process of the conceptual studies analysis. Field command manages a stock pile, but we establish and maintain the national nuclear weapon stock pile air base to provide weapons information for commanding control. War fighting capabilities assessment and capability. We also verify the custody of weapons through stock pile emergency verification. We control weapon movement and we manage the joints chief of staff nuclear weapons reserve."

Safety is the key element in all our business. Field commanders that are members in the surface nuclear weapons system safety groups. We provide technical advice on transportation and storage magazine construction and radiation safety. The list goes on and on. We are involved in nuclear weapons from cradle to grave as the saying goes. Things are changing fast, so fast that it is almost impossible for any one person or any one organization to assess it correctly. I can give you my views, though and I will. I think I can give you at least a basic feel for the dramatic transformation that is occurring as we speak."

There will be many changes, but tonight I will only talk about three changes that I see taking place in this nuclear community. First, and fundamentally the structure of the community is changing. I believe we are seeing a reversal of the trend towards decentralization that started in the early Sandio Base days. Some of you might remember Sandio Base. We now call it Kirkland Air Force Base and that's where I am now. All the program management of weapons, training, security, you name it was done centrally at Sandio Base. As events grew, the responsibilities shifted to the servicemen. The Army is moving out of the business, the Air Force is down sizing and tactical weapons have been removed from Navy ships. The nuclear community is shrinking so rapidly that the logistical aspect of weapons movement, storage and destruction are being pressured to keep pace."

The challenge we now face is the reversal of the decentralization that the current and the past twenty plus years witnessed. It is a tough challenge, but fortunately the infrastructure of making it happen is in place. As military planners, we never contemplated in our wildest dreams the events of the last two years. We are downsizing the stock pile as quickly and safely as possible and yet insuring that we maintain our nuclear capability as directed by the president, or our commander in chief."

The second change taking place is more increased emphasis on safety. What's more our weapons have better safe guards than sensitive high explosives for example. The point is simply this: while a nuclear detonation is unlikely, the focus is now to ensure against a fatal active material disbursement.

Appendix 4. Notes from the 50th Anniversary Banquet

And you can count on me to keep that from happening at least for another two months. Right now the department of defense is involved in efforts that we hope will lead to joint U.S. and Russian state involvement in the safety and security of their stock pile while they're still pointed at us."

Change three: you may have heard of President Nixon's new book, 'Seize the moment.' No matter what you think of him I think it is fair to say that this premise that the current situation with the Russians offers a historically unique opportunity. Personally, if we do not seize it, we will in all likelihood lose it. The fact is, we are a global super power. We are the only super power and maybe part of the reason is because of your dedication and sacrifice during World War II. We have global interests we cannot deny or *evade* these facts nor do we want to. Like it or not, other nations look at us for leadership not because they fear our power, but because they admire our values and they see us as the important force for peace and stability. Again, field command, my command, is making changes."

I believe that we must be ready for the changes that will continue to occur into the next century. We're dealing with change through a philosophy called total quality management. I call it total quality leadership. And that's what the chief of naval operations has also chosen for us to call it in the Navy, because I believe that management is a subset to leadership. Not the other way around."

In field command, total quality leadership is correctly using leadership, training and personnel management of our people to continuously improve quality to meet the needs of our customers. As commander, I have put my leadership on the line to propel field command and everyone else and in T.C. into the twenty first century for total quality. We cannot tolerate defects in our planet. We cannot say anymore that

80% good is good enough. We must stop inspecting to improve quality. That's too late, ineffective, costly. We must improve other plans during the plan stages so that tasks do not have problems in the implementation stage. We do not know exactly what the coming years will bring. In today's environment the service is already decreasing in size, but we are committed to take care of our people first while maintaining the highest standards and yes it can be done."

The emphasis on team work is even greater. The team must be strong and ready. In order for the team to be ready, individuals, all individuals, must be trained in the fundamental principles of total quality leadership (TQL). This applies to all of the departments of defense. Should apply everywhere in the country."

I will be more specific about the Navy; however, before I do that I am going to make a point that I'm having a joint command that is Army, Navy Air Force and Marines and I found out during this short assignment that it's quite different the way we do things in the Navy. When I first got there with my gold Navy format, I hit the deck place running, and I think you've heard that term before, you probably created it, and I saw probably fifty things that needed to be modified in the first fifteen days. And in my Navy fashion I started to order those things and everywhere I turned I saw an Air Force officer, I saw an Army officer. They'd say, 'Admiral you can't do that." I said, 'Stop me, and I want it finished by Friday.'"

There is another thing I learned, that different services have the same phrases that we do but they mean different things to them. Let me give you an example of what I mean. If you tell the Army to secure a building they go get a squad of tanks and a regiment of soldiers and surround the building and say we've got it secured. If you tell the Marine Corp to secure a building they go ahead and turn off all the lights and

Appendix 4. Notes from the 50th Anniversary Banquet

put a lock on the door and say the building is secure. If you tell the Air Force to go secure a building they go to the contract office and get a lease for two years from top to bottom."

So let's go back to the Navy: the United States Navy is ships, ladies and gentlemen, and then there's the sailors that go to sea, it is those who have mastered the art of seamanship. And I don't have to tell you about that end of Navy warfare and of command of fighting men at sea. The law has changed, but we don't have women on fighting ships yet. As it has so many times in history, you well know the Navy truly again came into it's own during Operation Desert Shield and Desert Storm; it delivered decisive orders against the enemy of naval gunfire, Navy air power and for the first time tunneled our missile. It guaranteed unchallenged use of sea lanes and then again showed witness to the President of Tripoli that Navy ships can absorb punishment and keep on fighting."

The list goes on and on and off hand it's very good, super in fact, because I'm here to tell you that the Navy's force is taking an increasingly vital roles in American National security as the new world era unfolds. This is why I think so. The two governing facts of life facing the Navy are these: first the Soviet. Union as a viable threat is gone. The Soviet Navy did not end up on the rocks when communists rule ended in Moscow. But the struggle that dominated our professional lives is now over. And Navy Secretary Garab says any plans for a peace time U.S. military based on cold war assumptions make neither strategic nor political sense. What is realistic is the assumption that the international community, whatever it is, will enlist us for its security, it's stability and it's confidence. America's determination is to stay engaged and to remain the underwriter of the democratic principles that we have struggled for a long time to defend. Bottom line; the U.S. Navy will visibly continue to protect power and influence anywhere in the world. You made sure of that. That's what combat-ready naval ships do better than anybody else for reasons that you know better than I."

No one else can provide flexible, visible, powerful yet unobtrusive combat-ready military presence like sailors and marines or Navy ships. Second fact, money, we need to decide quickly how to do business with as much as 25% less budget than we had in the 1980s. That we include all of government and industry in not just short term measures but rather in a permanent and fundamentally structuring of all our organizations and our thinking."

We must come to grips with the fact that our worlds have changed completely because pretending that they have not, pretending that we can continue to exist simply by keeping up old ways of doing things is the surest way to get tossed into history's dustpan. This is why. By the year 1995 nearly one million men and women will have been taken off the DOD payroll. All volunteer forces will be decreased by 520 thousand. We have over more than that in just this year. There will be 225 thousand fewer in the naval reserve; our reserve personnel. Civilian personnel will be decreased by 200 thousand. As another year past will be 80 thousand civilian jobs that have already been cut. In the past two years the department of defense has terminated over 100 plus programs. We must do it right."

What does that mean in practical terms? It means having a forward looking, realistic vision of where the Navy needs to be in the next ten to twenty years in terms of roles, missions, size, more structure, technology and tactics. It means investing our increasingly scarce resources where they will earn their maximum return on that vision. It means making lots of tough choices between what we would like to have and what we absolutely need to have. No matter what our world struc-

Appendix 4. Notes from the 50th Anniversary Banquet

ture, our strategy and our Navy ends up looking like; the one and only iron clad rule we have to remember is that they begin and end with people, smart dedicated, professionally satisfied men and women. Without them the finest hardware in the world is junk."

We need to resist and break temptation to break faith with our people and make hard decisions on their backs. We did that in 1976 and we should never do that again. The Navy has done a super job of matching policies to protect the infrastructure, but it's going to get tough. Some people are going to have to leave sooner than they want. It's already happened and nobody is happy about that. The process of thinning out could produce an even more competent and capable force of personnel in the future than we have now. Leadership is important when times are good, but it is virtually essential when things are confused, uncertain and anxious and things are certainly confused, uncertain and anxious right now. The Navy at every level has embraced total quality leadership. This country needs the Navy, you know that. And it's up to us, all of us, to make sure that America can count on another half century of unbeatable power at sea."

These changes which equal fleet readiness start right here at the naval training center, Great Lakes. And I'm looking forward again to continuing that correct positive impact on the great young people that we have out there; who you saw at yesterday's training. Changes are hard for people to accept."

Let me close by telling you a Navy story about a ship's captain who was unwilling to change; now that wasn't me. One especially dark night there was a Navy captain who went to the bridge of the ship. All he could see was a light coming straight at him. He watched it for a while and finally sent a message over saying, 'Change your course ten degrees to the north.' He got a message back, 'Change your course ten degrees to the south.' As all Navy captains like to give orders, he sent another message over saying, 'Change your course ten degrees to the north, this is the captain speaking.' He got a message back saying, 'Change your course ten degrees to the south. This is the officer of the watch.' This really made him mad. I can't say some of the words I'm thinking right now that he probably said. So he sent another message over saying, 'Change your course ten degrees to the north. This is a battleship.' He got a message back saying, 'Change your course ten degrees to the south, this is the lighthouse." So you see it is vital to know where you are and we in the Navy department of defense are changing our course to meet tomorrow's challenges and opportunities."

God bless all of you. Thank you."

We would like to present to you World War II Black Navy Veterans the Robert Smalls Achievement Award. It's something that's very, very dear to us. Most of us were in the Robert Smalls Camp in 1942, 43, 44, 45 and this is our way of saying thank you."

Fellows, there is something that I forgot to read yesterday when we were in Great Lakes. From the Secretary of the Navy":

5 June 1992.

Dear Mr. Colson: I regret very much that I will not be able to attend the historical event your organization is holding in Chicago on June 18–20. However, I hope you will pass to the members of World War II Black Navy Veterans Great Lakes my tremendous respect and congratulations for your heroic role in helping

Appendix 4. Notes from the 50th Anniversary Banquet

to create opportunities for Blacks in the United States Navy. The thousands of Black sailors serving their nation today have been able to succeed, at least in part, because of the courage and determination of Black veterans who went before them. We have come a great distance over the years in creating the Navy in which the color of a person's skin is not an impediment to his or her chance to serve. But the greatest distance was covered by those of you who took the first steps. You should all take enormous pride in what you've accomplished. I salute the Black Navy Veterans and I thank you for all you have done. I hope you will have many highly successful future anniversary celebration.

H. Longess Gary, III,
The Secretary of Navy.

Another one"

June 11, 1992.

Greetings from the office of mayorship of Chicago. As the mayor and on behalf of the City of Chicago I extend my cordial greetings to the Black World War II. Veterans gathering here in Chicago commemorating the fiftieth anniversary of Blacks being accepted in the general service of the United States Navy and Marine Corps. Chicagoans are both delighted and honored that you have chosen our city as the site of this anniversary. Your distinguished group of African-Americans is composed of former Navy personnel and marines who service our country at Camp Robert Smalls, Great Lakes, Illinois. As World War II Black Navy Veterans you've faced great hardships so that we might all live in freedom. Your sacrifice will never be forgotten nor our debt to you repaid. I salute you and extend my heartfelt gratitude for your selfless service. Today we remember and give great special thanks to those who lost their lives in the line of duty. Best wishes for a memorable anniversary and enjoyable visit. Please note that you will always be welcomed in Chicago.

Sincerely,
Richard M. Daley, Mayor

So with that note I would like to bring forth at this time another guest of our organization, Commander James Kendall."

"Good evening. I am surprised to be brought forth so as the Admiral mentioned, I will be very brief and then be seated. On behalf of the chief of naval operations in Washington and on behalf of the entire operating Navy staff Admiral Kelsey sends his greetings. He could not be here this evening because as I mentioned to some of the members yesterday he is presently in Russia meeting with the former Soviet Chief of Naval Operations and one of the things that they are talking about is some of the things that Admiral Gaston mentioned. He did call me in just before he left, though and reminded me that I was not to come here and embarrass the Navy. According to him we have one role and that's eating all the dessert. Again, I am grateful for the opportunity to share in the stories and learn some history. I say thank God for my opportunity

Appendix 4. Notes from the 50th Anniversary Banquet

and thank God and God Bless the World War II Black Navy Vets. Thank you."

"Thank you again. And now we'd like to introduce again Mrs. Jackie Pasco, my secretary Marcia. And now there's something that happened the other night. The membership had a raffle the other night and the winners were announced but had never come forward and I think I'd better announce them again."

THE LAST WORD

ARMED FORCES

Vice Adm. J. Paul Reason Becomes First Black Four-Star Admiral In The Navy

▲ President Bill Clinton recently nominated Vice Adm. J. Paul Reason for promotion to admiral and assignment as commander in chief of the U.S. Atlantic Fleet at Norfolk, VA.

Vice Adm. J. Paul Reason recently made history when he became the first Black promoted to the rank of four-star admiral in the U.S. Navy.

A native of Washington, D.C., Reason was nominated by President Bill Clinton for promotion to admiral and assignment as commander in chief of the U.S. Atlantic Fleet at Norfolk, VA, the Pentagon announced. The 55-year-old, four-star admiral is currently deputy chief of naval operations for plans, policy and operation in the Pentagon.

If confirmed by the Senate as expected, Reason will replace Adm. William J. Flanagan as head of the Atlantic Fleet. Flanagan is considered a candidate to replace Marine Gen. John J. Sheehan as commander in chief of the U.S. Atlantic Command.

In 1975, the late Daniel (Chappie) James became the first Black four-star U.S. Air Force general, and the late Roscoe Robinson Jr. became the first Black four-star U.S. Army general in 1982. The U.S. Marine Corps has never had a Black four-star officer.

Reason, who graduated from the U.S. Naval Academy at Annapolis, commanded surface ships in the Atlantic, served aboard the *USS Enterprise* and was a naval aide to former President Jimmy Carter.

From *Jet*, June 3rd, 1996

The Author

James S. Peters, II received his Ph.D. in counseling and clinical psychology from Purdue University where he was a Veterans Administration Fellow and Research Associate. His undergraduate degree was completed at Southern University, Baton Rouge, Louisiana. At Southern he was a T. H. Harris Scholarship Fellow, Captain, and Little All-American football player. He holds a Master of Arts Degree in Social Psychology from the Hartford Seminary Foundation; Master of Science Degree, Clinical Psychology, Illinois Institute of Technology; and has done graduate work in Psychology at the University of Chicago, where he was a clinical psychology intern in the Veterans Administration program. At the present time he is an independent practitioner of psychology. For 25 years he was Associate Commissioner, Division of Vocational Rehabilitation and Disability Determination, Connecticut State Department of Education; Adjunct Professor, Department of Psychology, University of Hartford; and Lecturer on rehabilitation, Department of Educational Psychology, University of Connecticut. Dr. Peters is a licensed psychologist in the states of Connecticut, New York, New Hampshire, California, Massachusetts, and Vermont, and Certified in Louisiana. During 1971-1973 he was a Postdoctoral Research Fellow, Harvard University, School of Medicine, Department of Psychiatry, and a Special Fellow in the U.S., Department of Health, Education, and Welfare, Social and Rehabilitation Services, while studying rehabilitation in the United States and Europe. In 1976 and 1977 he studied rehabilitation needs in West Africa and Brazil.

Index

A

Allen, Milton B. 48, 50
Arbor, Jesse 31, 109, 138
Armstrong, Commander D.W. 2, 3, 5, 7, 27, 29, 30, 51

B

Bacon, Theodell 109
Baker, Harry J. 109
Bard, Ralph A. 11
Barnes, Samuel 73
Barnes, Phillip 73
Beethoven, Ludwig von 85, 90
Belle, Mr. amd Mrs. Herman 90, 97
Belle, Mr. Herman 95, 98
Bledsoe, George Matthew 96
Bond, Captain 5, 6
Bowden, Len 120
Bowman, Arthur M. 109
Bowman, Russel 86
Bradford, Nelson 92
Branch, London 120
Bridge, Thomas 120
Brooks, Clay 101, 102
Brough, Dr. Edmund 88
Brough, Mrs. Zeila 88
Brown, James 85
Brown, Lt. James 73
Burrell, Charles 93, 96
Byrne, Jane M. 117

C

Calloway, Cab 99
Calloway, Jerome 99
Cananzie, Milburn 38
Carter, James R. 109
Carter, Warrick 120
Chaney, Dr. Henry 26
Chew, Charles, Jr. 107, 109, 125
Clinton, Phillip 46
Collins, Lieutenant Gerald 126
Colson, Secretary of the Navy 148
Colston, Leroy 40
Cook, Carson 109
Cook, Culbreth B. 109
Cooper, Jerome S. 109
Cummings, Dr. S.B. 28
Curtis, Harry 92

D

Daley, Mayor Richard M. 150
Davis, Commander C.A. 113
Davis, James 109
Dermody, William B. 119
Derr, Gilbert 109
Downs, Commander 36, 43, 44

E

Emory, Commodore T.R.M. 138
Emmett, Commodore 5, 6

157

F

Fambro, Anthony 104
Ferguson, Marie E. *(see Marie Peters)* ix
Flatley, Rear Admiral James H. 108, 118
Flowers, Captain 27
Floyd, Dr. Samuel A., Jr. 8, 56, 92, 94, 97, 98, 99, 103, 104, 120
Forrestal, James 11
Foster, Dudley 102
Francois, Clarence 92, 93
Freem, Captain 6
Funderburg, Howard 120

G

Gaston, Admiral Mark C. 40, 139, 150
Goodwin, Reginald 27, 28, 73
Goodrich, James F. 113
Granger, Lester 11
Gravely, Admiral Samuel L 43, 44, 115, 118, 140
Greenough, Billie 26
Greenough, Evelyn 26
Greenough, Mrs. Charlotte 25
Greer, Robert S. 109
Griffin, James S. 109
Griffin, Johnny 26
Guiness, Luther 98

H

Hale, Richard 87
Haley, Richard 103
Hall, Marshall 96
Harper, Clifford D. 56
Hayes, Alvin 109
Hill, Clinton 109
Hill, Crackton 43, 44
Hill, Dr. Floyd 90
Holley, Major 120
Holyhue, Major 93
Homer, Billy 94
Hopes, Chief 102
Howard, James T. xi, 39, 52, 55, 57, 58, 106–110, 112–115, 118, 121, 124–128, 138
Howard, Hayward 46
Hume, Diane Spencer, xi
Hunt, Dr. William 28

I

Irvin, Bernard J. 109

J

Jackson, Roy 57
Jackson, Rudy 32, 34
Jarrett, Vernon 109, 124
Jellon, Jedd 88
Johnson, Douglas W. 109
Johnson, Louis C. 20, 73, 109
Johnson, Lyman T. 109
Joker, Anonymous 47
Jones, Mark E. 108, 109, 127, 128
Jones, Sam 94

K

Kendall, Commander James 139, 150
King, Dr. Martin Luther 31, 38

L

Lee, James O. 109
Lightfoot, James 92
Lofton, Robert W. 109
Lord, Melvin E., Jr. 92

Index

Luthsmall, Nick 91
Lynn, Lieutenant 28

M

Macy, Janet xi, 58
Mareno, Chief Petty Officer 29, 30
Marshall, Leonard 109
Marshall, Thurgood 10, 11
Martin, Henry A. 109
Matthews, James M. 109
McBean, P.J. 15
Meir, Golda 140
Miller, Howard 89
Miller, Dorie 40
Mines, Walter xi, 56, 57, 86, 97
Moore, Malvin E. 56, 103

N

Nabastagget, Commander 44
Nelson, Dennis 5, 8, 28, 46, 73
Nixon, Richard M. 143
Norman, Noble 109

O

Owens, Lieutenant Paul 126

P

Palace, Stanley 91
Parham, Thomas 73
Parsons, Judge 127
Pasco, Jackie 151
Patterson, Cardovus T. 109, 110
Peabody, Annie 102
Penn, Nathan 126
Penning, Sammy Louis 92
Penny, Captain 6
Perkins, Dr. Huel D., Sr. xi, 56, 87, 97, 120

Perkins, Mrs. Robert 25
Perkins, Robert 25
Pest, Skeeter 94
Peters, Ardell 25
Peters, James S., II x, 27, 39, 48, 51–53, 55, 58, 70, 106, 108, 109, 116, 117, 121, 125–128, 155
Peters, Marie *(see Marie Ferguson)* 26
Pillars, Charles 120
Pillars, Hayes 120
Pittman, C.E. 87, 88
Polk, George D., II 109
Poole, James W. 109
Poole, Julius 89
Prince, Mason 88, 89

R

Reagan, Ronald 57
Reason, Admiral Paul 139
Relionzak, Jack 91
Robertson, Judd 86
Rhoden, H.S. 109
Roller, Morris L. 109
Roosevelt, Franklin D. 1, 53, 107, 140
Ross, Fred 41, 42

S

Smalls, Robert 148
Smith, Dr. and Mrs. Robert G. 26
Smith, Francis 26
Smith, William W. 109
Steele, David 26
Stuart, Vincent C. 109
Suprenaunt, Dennis 91

T

Taylor, Vulcan E. 58, 108, 109, 121, 124
Terry, Clark 101, 103, 104, 120
Thomas, William 27, 52
Thompson, Arthur 73
Thompson, James R. 116, 125
Tie, Meril 89
Trice, Clarence 102, 103
Trump, Miss 88
Tucker, Rufus 95, 120
Tyree, Spottswood L. 109

V

Vaughns, Wyman 36, 88, 108, 109, 124–126

W

Wallace, Bobby J. 109
Washington, Harold 125
Washington, Jack 88
Watkins, Admiral James D. 111
Weinberger, Caspar 112, 114
White, Clarence N. 109
White, Walter 13, 14
Wilkins, (Eddy) 100
Wilkins, Ernie 120
Wilkins, Etson 109
Wilkins, Jimmy 120
Williams, Charles 39, 87
Williams, Lewis R. (Nummy) 27, 51, 109, 124, 125
Wilson, Kenneth O. 109
Wolf, Chief Petty Officer 24
Womack, Captain 139, 141
Wood, Mitchell (Booty) 94, 120
Wright, Rear Admiral Carleton 10

Y

Yepan, Charles Jr. 31

www.ingramcontent.com/pod-product-compliance
Lightning Source LLC
Chambersburg PA
CBHW070642300426
44111CB00013B/2215